KINGS & QUEENS

1,000 YEARS OF BRITISH ROYALTY

CONTENTS

A TRAGIC AFFAIR

Lady Jane Grey was the cousin and childhood sweetheart of Edward VI. When he realised he was dying, he decided that she should rule after his death instead of his half-sister, Mary. She came to the throne at 16 and ruled for just nine days, before relinquishing the crown to Mary. She was later beheaded for treason.

IMPORTANT EVENTS

Look out for the following symbols through this book, highlighting key events of our past

- ARCHITECTURE
- ARTS & LITERATURE
- EXPLORATION
- FAMOUS BATTLES
- GOVERNMENT
- HEALTH & MEDICINE
- JUSTICE
- RELIGION
- SCIENCE

THE ROYAL FAMILY TREE

KINGS & QUEENS OF SCOTLAND·LINE OF SUCCESSION

KENNETH MACALPIN - 834-859
DONALD I - 859-863
CONSTANTINE I - 863-877
AEDH - 877-878
EOCHA - 878-889
DONALD II - 889-900
CONSTANTINE II - 900-942
MALCOLM I - 942-954
INDULPHUS - 954-962
DUFF - 962-967
CUILEAN - 967-971
KENNETH II - 971-995
CONSTANTINE III - 995-997
KENNETH III - 997-1005
MALCOLM II - 1005-1034
DUNCAN I - 1034-1040

MACBETH - 1040-1057
LULACH - 1057-1058
MALCOLM III - 1058-1093
DONALD III - 1093-1094
  & 1094-1097
DUNCAN II - 1094
EDGAR - 1097-1107
ALEXANDER I - 1107-1124
DAVID I - 1124-1153
MALCOLM IV - 1153-1165
WILLIAM THE LION - 1165-1214
ALEXANDER II - 1214-1249
ALEXANDER III - 1249-1286
MARGARET OF NORWAY - 1286-90
JOHN BALLIOL - 1292-96 (Edward I
  of England - 1296-1306)

ROBERT I (Bruce) - 1306-1329
DAVID II (Bruce) - 1329-1332
EDWARD BALLIOL - 1332-56
DAVID II (Bruce) - 1356-1371
ROBERT II - 1371-1390
ROBERT III - 1390-1406
JAMES I - 1406-1437
JAMES II - 1437-1460
JAMES III - 1460-1488
JAMES IV - 1488-1513
JAMES V - 1513-1542
MARY - 1542-1567
JAMES VI - 1567-1625
  (who became James I of England
  and the countries were united)

THE NORMANS 1066 – 1154

⚜ WILLIAM I 1066–1087 *m* Matilda of Flanders

⚜ WILLIAM II 1087-1100

⚜ HENRY I 1100-1135
  m Matilda of Scotland

MATILDA *m*
Geoffrey, Count of Anjou

ADELA
  m Stephen, Count of Blois

⚜ STEPHEN 1135-1154

THE PLANTAGENETS 1154 – 1399

⚜ HENRY II 1154-1189 *m* Eleanor of Aquitaine

⚜ RICHARD I 1189-1199

⚜ JOHN 1199–1216 *m* Isabel of Angouleme

⚜ HENRY III 1216–1272 *m* Eleanor of Provence

⚜ EDWARD I 1272-1307 *m* Eleanor of Castile

⚜ EDWARD II 1307-1327 *m* Isabella of France

⚜ EDWARD III 1327-1377 *m* Philippa of Hainault

EDWARD PRINCE OF WALES
(The Black Prince) *m* Joan of Kent

⚜ RICHARD II 1377-1399

JOHN OF GAUNT *m1* Blanche of Lancaster   *m2* Constance of Castile
                                           m3 Katharine Swynford

JOHN BEAUFORT Earl of Somerset

JOHN BEAUFORT Duke of Somerset

EDMUND *m* Owen Tudor   *m2* Owen Tudor
TUDOR

THE HOUSE OF LANCASTER 1399 -1461

⚜ HENRY IV 1399-1413 *m* Mary de Bohun

⚜ HENRY V 1413-1422 *m1* Katherine of France

⚜ HENRY VI 1422-1471

EDWARD, PRINCE OF WALES

EDMUND DUKE OF YORK

RICHARD, EARL OF CAMBRIDGE

RICHARD DUKE OF YORK

THE HOUSE OF YORK 1461 - 1485

⚜ EDWARD IV 1461-1483   ⚜ RICHARD III 1483-1485

⚜ EDWARD V

EDMUND *m* Margaret
TUDOR   Beaufort

THE TUDORS 1485-1603

⚜ HENRY VII *m* Elizabeth
  1485-1509   of York

MARGARET TUDOR *m* James IV of Scotland

4

JAMES V OF SCOTLAND *m* Mary of Guise

MARY QUEEN OF SCOTS *m* Henry Stuart

🜍 HENRY VIII 1509-1547
m1 Catherine of Aragon (*div* 1533)
m2 Anne Boleyn (*d.1536*)
m3 Jane Seymour (*d.1537*)
m4 Anne of Cleeves (*div 1540*)
m5 Catherine Howard (*d. 1542*)
m6 Catherine Parr (*d. 1548*)

🜍 MARY I 1553-1558
🜍 ELIZABETH I 1558-1603
🜍 EDWARD VI 1547-1553

THE STUARTS 1603-1714

🜍 JAMES I (*VI of Scotland*) 1603-1625 *m* Anne of Denmark

HENRY FREDRICK, PRINCE OF WALES *d.1612*

🜍 CHARLES I 1625-1649 *m* Henrietta Maria of France *d. 1669*

ELIZABETH *d.1662* *m* Frederick V, Elector Palatine of the Rhine

RUPERT OF THE RHINE *d.1682*

SOPHIA *d.1612 m* Ernest Augustus, Elector of Hanover *d.1698*

MARY *m* William, Prince of Orange

🜍 CHARLES II 1649-1685 *m* Catherine of Braganza *d.1705*

🜍 JAMES II 1685-1688 *d. 1701 m* Anne Hyde *d.1671*

🜍 WILLIAM III 1689-1702
🜍 MARY II 1689-1694

🜍 ANNE 1702-1714 *m* George of Denmark

THE HANOVARIANS 1714 - 1910

🜍 GEORGE I 1714-1727 *m* Sophia Dorothea of Zelle *d.1726*

🜍 GEORGE II 1727-1760 *m* Caroline of Anspach *d.1737*

FREDERICK LEWIS, PRINCE OF WALES *d.1751 m* Augusta of Saxe-Gotha *d.1772*

🜍 GEORGE III 1760-1820 *m* Sophia Charlotte of Mecklenburg-Strelitz *d.1818*

🜍 GEORGE IV 1820-1830 *m* Caroline of Brunswick

CHARLOTTE *d.1817*

🜍 WILLIAM IV 1830-1837 *m* Adelaide of Saxe-Meiningen 1792-1849

CHARLOTTE *d.1819*

ELIZABETH *d.1821*

EDWARD, DUKE OF KENT *d.1820 m* Victoria of Saxe-Coburg-Saalfeld *d.1861*

🜍 VICTORIA 1837-1901 *m* Albert of Saxe-Coburg-Gotha, Prince Consort *d.1861*

🜍 EDWARD VII 1901-1910

THE HOUSE OF WINDSOR 1910-

🜍 GEORGE V 1910-1936

🜍 GEORGE VI 1936-1952 *m* Elizabeth Bowes-Lyon

🜍 EDWARD VIII, DUKE OF WINDSOR 1936 (*d.1972*)

🜍 ELIZABETH II 1952-

KINGS & QUEENS OF ENGLAND
(Britain from 1603) LINE OF SUCCESSION

ECGBERHT - 827-839
AETHELWULF - 839-866
AETHELRED I - 866-871
ALFRED THE GREAT - 871-900
EDWARD THE ELDER - 900-924
ATHELSTAN - 924-940
EDMUND I - 940-946
EADRED I - 946-955
EDWY - 955-959
EADGAR THE PEACEABLE - 959-975
EDWARD THE MARTYR - 975-978
AETHELRED II - 978-1013 & 1014-1016
SWEYN (*Dane*) - 1013-1014
EDMUND IRONSIDE - 1016
CANUTE (*Dane*) - 1016-1035
HAROLD HAREFOOT (*Dane*) - 1035-1040
HARTHACANUTE (*Dane*) - 1040-1042
EDWARD THE CONFESSOR - 1042-1066
HAROLD II - 1066
WILLIAM I (*the Conqueror*) - 1066-1087
WILLIAM II - 1087-1100
HENRY I - 1100-1135
STEPHEN - 1135-1154
HENRY II - 1154-1189
RICHARD I - 1189-1199
JOHN - 1199-1216
HENRY III - 1216-1272
EDWARD I - 1272-1307

EDWARD II - 1307-1327
EDWARD III - 1327-1377
RICHARD II - 1377-1399
HENRY IV - 1399-1413
HENRY V - 1413-1422
HENRY VI - 1422-1471
EDWARD IV - 1461-1483
EDWARD V - 1483
RICHARD III - 1483-1485
HENRY VII - 1485-1509
HENRY VIII - 1509-1547
EDWARD VI - 1547-1553
MARY I - 1553-1558
ELIZABETH I - 1558-1603
JAMES I - 1603-1625
CHARLES I - 1625-1649
CHARLES II - 1649-1685
JAMES II - 1685-1688
WILLIAM III & MARY II - 1689-1702
ANNE - 1702-1714
GEORGE I - 1714-1727
GEORGE II - 1727-1760
GEORGE III - 1760-1820
GEORGE IV - 1820-1830
WILLIAM IV - 1830-1837
VICTORIA - 1837-1901
EDWARD VII - 1901-1910
GEORGE V - 1910-1936
EDWARD VIII - 1936
GEORGE VI - 1936-1952
ELIZABETH II - 1952-today

AETHELRED THE UNREADY (978-1016)

Aethelred was a weak monarch who tried to buy off the Vikings by paying them money, known as the Danegeld, raised from taxes. It was an unpopular and ineffective measure that forced him to flee the country.

A DANISH KING

Following the death of Alfred, England remained at war with the Viking invaders for the next 150 years. Peace came under the strong and wise leadership of Canute, a Dane, who was crowned king of England, Denmark and Norway (1016-35). Canute was said to be so powerful that he could command the waves, a claim he vehemently denied, as shown above.

LINE OF SUCCESSION

Saxon & Danish Kings

Ecgberht - 827-839
Aethelwulf - 839-866
Aethelred I - 866-871
Alfred the Great - 871-899
Edward the Elder - 899-925
Athelstan- 925-939
Edmund I - 939-946
Eadred I - 946-959
Eadgar the Peaceable - 959-975
Edward the Martyr - 975-978
Aethelred II - 978-1013 & 1014-1016
Sweyn (Dane) - 1013-1014
Edmund Ironside (Dane) - 1016
Canute (Dane) - 1016-1035
Harold Harefoot (Dane) - 1035-1040
Harthacanute (Dane) - 1040-1042
Edward the Confessor - 1042-1066
Harold II - 1066

EARLY KINGS
SAXON & DANISH KINGS (up to 1066)

*U*ntil the 9th century, Britain was a divided land with many separate kingdoms. The area we now know as England was first unified under the rule of Ecgberht (827–39) but peace did not last. Alfred the Great finally united the nation and ruled over all England from 886 until his death in 899. Succession to the throne in Saxon England was far from being a formality, passing automatically from father to eldest son. The crown was frequently wrested by acts of violence on the battlefield or even by murder. For a brief period in the early 11th century, England was ruled by Danish kings. In 1066 the Normans (or Norse-men) who were also of Scandinavian descent, claimed the English crown. They brought stability to the throne and from then on began the modern system of numbering the monarchs.

EADGAR THE PEACEABLE

Eadgar the Peaceable came to the throne in 959 and the following year installed Dunstan as Archbishop of Canterbury. He was known as the 'Peaceable' because his reign was one of prosperity and relative peace with the Vikings. Eadgar also divided the shires into smaller units of administration known as hundreds, each with its own court.

ECGBERHT (827-39)

First King of All England
In 802 Ecgberht became King of Wessex, which soon became the most powerful of the Saxon kingdoms. In 827 the other six kings swore allegiance to him and he became the first true king of a united England.

ARCHITECTURE   ARTS & LITERATURE   EXPLORATION   FAMOUS BATTLES

EDWARD – A PIOUS KING (1042–66)

Edward (above), known as the Confessor because of his pious nature, proved to be a strong king, though his preference for Norman advisers incurred the wrath of the Saxon nobility and led, eventually, to the conquest of England by the Normans.

✞ THE VENERABLE BEDE

The first proper English history book, the 'Ecclesiastical History of the English Nation', was written by Bede (673-735) a Saxon monk from the monasteries of Monkwearmouth and Jarrow, in the kingdom of Northumbria.

📖 ANGLO SAXON CHRONICLE

In 891 Alfred the Great instigated the compilation of the Anglo-Saxon Chronicle in an attempt to record the history of his newly unified nation. Written in Anglo-Saxon, instead of Latin, it gives a brief social and political history of England from before the Roman occupation to the Norman conquest.

🏛 WESTMINSTER ABBEY

The original Westminster Abbey was founded in the 7th century and rebuilt by Edward the Confessor between 1052-65. Rebuilt again by Henry III after 1272 additions were made right up to the 18th century. The Benedictine abbey itself was dissolved by Henry VIII in 1540 but the magnificent church remains. Most English monarchs have been crowned at the abbey and many are buried there.

ALFRED THE GREAT (871–99)

Alfred succeeded to the throne of Wessex in 871 and immediately set about reducing the Danish threat. It is whilst Alfred was in hiding in Somerset that he is supposed to have burned the cakes left in his charge, whilst plotting against the Danes. Despite early defeats, he eventually forced the Danes to sign a treaty at Wedmore in 878 confining them to an area north of the Wash, known as Danelaw. In 886 Alfred finally defeated the Danes at London and was recognised as King of all England.

KING OFFA (757–96)

For long, the most powerful of the Saxon kingdoms was Mercia, under the able rule of Offa. The Celtic people of what is now Wales, to the west, were a constant threat so Offa had a huge defensive earthwork, known as Offa's Dyke, constructed to protect his lands, much of which still survives today.

The Seven Kingdoms

Scotland

Northumbria

☐ *Occupied by Britons*

— *Boundaries of Kingdoms*

North Wales

Mercia

North Folk
East Anglia
South Folk

West Wales

Wessex

Essex

Kent

Sussex

THE KINGDOMS OF ENGLAND

From the departure of the Romans until about 827 England was divided into seven separate kingdoms, known as the Heptarchy, as shown on this map. Scotland, Wales and Ireland were also separate kingdoms in their own right.

📜 GOVERNMENT　　⚕ HEALTH & MEDICINE　　⚖ JUSTICE　　✞ RELIGION　　🗒 SCIENCE

THE BATTLE OF HASTINGS
CLAIMANTS TO THE THRONE

THE INVASION FLEET

During the course of 1066 Duke William assembled a huge fleet of ships to transport his army of 4,000 infantry and 3,000 cavalry, together with their horses and supplies, across the Channel. He landed at Pevensey Bay, on the Sussex coast, and then moved on to Hastings.

HASTINGS CASTLE

William transported prefabricated timber panels in his invasion fleet, which he used to construct a temporary castle on the cliffs at Hastings. The Bayeux Tapestry shows clearly the Normans digging ditches and constructing the mound for this, one of the first motte and bailey castles in England.

Edward the Confessor was half-Norman and, until the age of 35, lived with his mother in Normandy. After he became king he often surrounded himself with Norman advisers and in 1051 he promised the English throne to Duke William of Normandy. On his deathbed, however, Edward stated that his brother-in-law, Harold Godwinson, Earl of Wessex, should be king. Harold had previously (in 1064) sworn allegiance to Duke William, so when he was crowned king William declared his intention to invade England and take the throne by force.

BATTLE ABBEY

Following his victory, William vowed to build an abbey on the site of the battle. Begun soon after, it was not completed until 1094, seven years after the Conqueror's death. Greatly extended in later centuries, much of the abbey still survives today.

HAROLD GODWINSON

Harold was the son of Godwin, Earl of Wessex, whose sister Edith married the king, Edward the Confessor. An ongoing dispute eventually led, in 1051, to the Godwin family being banished from England. They were restored to their estates the following year and in 1053 Harold became the king's chief adviser. He persuaded Edward to renege on his promise to pass the crown to Duke William and had himself proclaimed king on Edward's death on 5th January 1066.

597
St. Augustine arrives in Canterbury and begins conversion of people to Christianity.

731
Bede completes his 'Ecclesiastical History of the English Nation', the first history book of England.

780
Offa's Dyke begun, defensive ditch between England and Wales.
787
First Viking raids

of England begin.
825
Ecgberht of Wessex defeats king of Mercia.
827
Ecgberht becomes first

King of all England.
871
Alfred the Great becomes king of Wessex.
878
Treaty of Wedmore

ARCHITECTURE   ARTS & LITERATURE   EXPLORATION   FAMOUS BATTLES

📖 BAYEUX TAPESTRY

Odo, Bishop of Bayeux and half brother of Duke William, is believed to have commissioned the Bayeux Tapestry, a huge needlework tableau (shown far left and below) depicting the events leading up to, and following, the Battle of Hastings, as part of the victory celebrations. Several scenes from the tapestry are shown here.

💣 BATTLE OF STAMFORD BRIDGE

William's invasion consisted of a two-pronged attack. While he slipped across the Channel unopposed, Harold Hardrada, king of Norway, launched an attack in the north. Harold Godwinson (of England) defeated the Norwegians at the Battle of Stamford Bridge in Yorkshire. The weary Saxons then had to march 250 miles south to meet William and the Normans encamped in Sussex.

THE BATTLE

The battle took place on 14th October 1066 about six miles north of Hastings on an escarpment known as Senlac Hill. Both armies were evenly matched, though the Saxons were tired from their long march south following the Battle of Stamford Bridge. The Saxons occupied the top of the ridge and successfully held off the Norman advances. Late in the day, William ordered his men to feign a retreat. The Saxons gave chase and lost the advantage of the high ground, leaving them at the mercy of the Norman archers and cavalry. The Normans were victorious and though Harold sustained a fatal injury, it is not now certain that he actually died on the battlefield. The above is a late 15th century illustration of the Battle of Hastings.

WILLIAM OF NORMANDY

The Normans, or 'Norsemen', were originally Vikings who settled in an area of northern France in the early 10th century. They built up a powerful domain, ruled by a duchy, rivalling the power of the king of France. William was the illegitimate son of Robert, Duke of Normandy, and he succeeded to the dukedom in 1035 when only 8 years old. He greatly extended his empire to much of western Europe and is said never to have engaged in a fight he did not win.

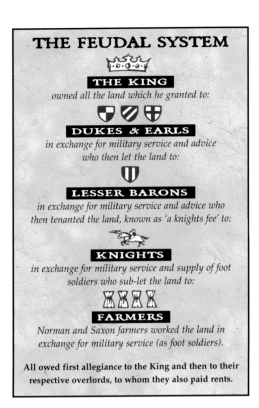

THE FEUDAL SYSTEM

THE KING
owned all the land which he granted to:

DUKES & EARLS
*in exchange for military service and advice
who then let the land to:*

LESSER BARONS
*in exchange for military service and advice who
then tenanted the land, known as 'a knights fee' to:*

KNIGHTS
*in exchange for military service and supply of foot
soldiers who sub-let the land to:*

FARMERS
*Norman and Saxon farmers worked the land in
exchange for military service (as foot soldiers).*

**All owed first allegiance to the King and then to their
respective overlords, to whom they also paid rents.**

THE FEUDAL SYSTEM

One of the first things William did on becoming king was to reorganise the governmental structure of England with the introduction of the feudal system. Basically, all land was held by the king and sub-tenanted to his most loyal lords. They in turn sub-let their holdings and so on, down to tenant farmers. All owed allegiance to their immediate overlord, and ultimately the king, who could call upon them at any time to do military service.

📖 THE DOMESDAY BOOK

In 1085 William ordered the compilation of a great survey of his newly conquered land. Completed in just one year and covering most of the country, it records in minute detail the land ownership and uses of almost every village and estate. The population of England at that time was recorded as two million. Compiled in two huge volumes, the Domesday Book (right) still exists today.

THE ROYAL FORESTS

In medieval times the word 'forest' simply meant an area set aside for hunting and included woodland and open land. By the end of the 12th century about one-third of England had been designated royal forest. One of the first of these was the New Forest in Hampshire in 1079. Severe forest laws were introduced to protect the game for hunting.

THE HARRYING OF THE NORTH

In the years immediately following the Conquest several rebellions broke out against Norman rule, the most serious being in the north of England. William responded with a 'scorched earth' policy, burning and laying waste huge areas of the north to quash the rebellion.

MOTTE & BAILEY CASTLES

William was able to hold down his newly conquered lands in England with the help of castles, the private fortified residences of his barons. Early castles were constructed of earth and timber for speed and consisted of a mound, or motte, surmounted by a wooden tower, with a courtyard, or bailey, attached, the whole thing protected by ditches and timber palisades. When time and money allowed, the timber defences were replaced with strong stone walls. The castle above is the motte and bailey at York.

1064
Harold Godwinson swears an oath of allegiance to William of Normandy.
1066
Edward the Confessor

dies and is succeeded by Harold Godwinson.
1066
Duke William of Normandy invades

England to claim throne.
1066
Battle of Hastings - William of Normandy defeats Harold and becomes king as William I.

1068/9
Harrying of the North.
1070
Lanfranc appointed

Archbishop of Canterbury.
1070
Canterbury Cathedral destroyed by fire. Lanfranc begins building

🏛 ARCHITECTURE   📖 ARTS & LITERATURE   ⚑ EXPLORATION   ⬥ FAMOUS BATTLES

WILLIAM I
BORN 1027 • ACCEDED 1066 • DIED 1087

*W*illiam was the illegitimate son of Robert, Duke of Normandy, who inherited that title at the age of eight. He had been promised the English throne in 1051 by Edward the Confessor, whose mother was of Norman descent. When Edward later went back on his word and promised succession to his brother-in-law Harold Godwinson, William decided to take the throne by force. After the battle William subdued the Saxons by confiscating their land and giving it to his Norman supporters. He was a fair if sometimes brutal ruler and died after falling from his horse during a military campaign in France.

CORONATION

Following his victory at Hastings, on 14th October 1066, William then marched on London, putting down local opposition as he went. He was crowned on Christmas Day the same year in Westminster Abbey.

ROYAL FORTRESS

The Tower of London was begun in 1078 when William ordered its construction, in stone. It soon became the principal royal residence and prison and has been added to in every century since then. The original mound was known (at least from the 6th century) as the 'White Mount', from where the 'White Tower' takes its name and not, as is popularly supposed, from being painted white in the Middle Ages, as many castles were.

SAXON REBELLION

Hereward the Wake led a Saxon rebellion against the Normans from his secret hideaway in the marshes surrounding the Isle of Ely, in Cambridgeshire. William defeated the rebels in 1071.

BISHOP ODO

Odo was William I's half-brother and came across with the Conqueror in 1066. He was created Earl of Kent and later Bishop of Bayeux, although he was always more interested in acquiring land and power than in affairs of the church. He led an unsuccessful rebellion against William and was banished from England in 1082.

---

to a much larger plan.
1071
Hereward the Wake (leader of Saxon revolt against Normans) is defeated.

1072
William I invades Scotland and wins homage from Malcolm III.
1077/8
Work begins on the

Tower of London, one of the earliest stone castles built in England.
1079
New Forest in Hampshire

enclosed for royal hunting.
1080
William refuses to pay homage to the pope.
1085
Domesday Book, a survey

of all land holdings, is begun.
1087
William I dies in a horse riding accident during siege of Nantes.

📜 GOVERNMENT   ⚗ HEALTH & MEDICINE   ⚖ JUSTICE   ✝ RELIGION   📋 SCIENCE

WILLIAM II

BORN 1056(?) • ACCEDED 1087 • DIED 1100

A CORRUPT BULLY

William held a lascivious court and openly extracted money from the church, but it was the actions of his mercenary soldiers that attracted most criticism. Villagers were said to desert their homes when the king's entourage approached rather than submit to their brutality.

When William I died, his lands were divided amongst his two eldest sons, Robert, who inherited Normandy, and William, who became king of England. Although, as invaders, none of the Norman kings were popular with the Saxons, William I had at least been a strong and just ruler. His son William, known as 'Rufus' because of the reddish colour of his hair and complexion, was more ruthless and less judicial than his father. He never married and on his death the throne passed to his younger brother, Henry.

ANSELM

When Lanfranc, the Archbishop of Canterbury, died the position fell vacant for four years. William installed Anselm, a Benedictine monk from France, in 1093 but he rowed with the king over high taxation and was forced into exile in 1097. Three years later Henry I recalled him to power.

A HUNTING ACCIDENT?

William was killed, supposedly, in a hunting accident in the New Forest on 2nd August 1100. A chance arrow, fired by Walter Tyrell, glanced off a tree and struck the king, although it has been suggested his brother Henry, as heir to the throne, may have given orders for his assassination. The 'Rufus Stone' marks the spot in the forest today.

1087
William I's second eldest son becomes William II of England, his eldest son Robert succeeds as Duke of Normandy.

1088
William defeats rebellion led by his uncle, Bishop Odo in Normandy in support of Robert's claim

to the throne.
1090
William leads unsuccessful invasion of Normandy

1092
Cumberland captured

from Scotland and annexed to England.
1093
Anselm becomes Archbishop of Canterbury.

1093
Malcolm III of Scotland invades England and is killed in the process.

🏛 ARCHITECTURE   📖 ARTS & LITERATURE   ⤷ EXPLORATION   ◆ FAMOUS BATTLES

WESTMINSTER HALL

William ordered the construction of Westminster Hall in 1097 on the site of an earlier palace. The great hammerbeam roof was added in the 1390s. It remained the principal royal residence until Henry VIII's reign, but most of the buildings burned down in 1834. The Houses of Parliament now occupy much of the site.

INVASION BY SCOTLAND

Malcolm III of Scotland invaded England on five separate occasions in an attempt to annex the counties of Northumberland, Cumberland and Westmorland to Scotland. The last time was in 1093 when he was killed by William II at the Battle of Alnwick.

⛪ DURHAM CATHEDRAL

The present cathedral (above) was begun in 1093 and remains one of the finest Norman buildings in the country. It contains the body of St. Cuthbert, a seventh century Celtic monk, whose tomb was a centre of pilgrimage throughout the Middle Ages.

THE BARONS' REVOLT

William's brother Robert laid claim to the English throne and led a baronial revolt against him, supported by their uncle, Bishop Odo. William crushed the revolt in 1088 and another, in Northumberland, in 1095.

THE ROYAL SPORT

The Norman kings enjoyed hunting, almost to the point of obsession, and gave over large tracts of land for the pursuit. Stags were popular quarry, as were wolves and wild boar, which were not yet extinct in England.

1095
William puts down a baronial revolt in Northumbria.

1095
Pope Urban II calls

a 'holy war' to recover the Holy Lands from the Muslims.

1096/7
First crusade to the Holy Lands regains

Jerusalem, but success is short lived.

1097
Anselm exiled to Rome and all his estates forfeited to crown.

1097
William begins construction of Westminster Hall.

1098
Welsh rebellion

against Norman rule put down.

1100
William II is killed in a hunting accident in the New Forest.

📜 GOVERNMENT ⚗ HEALTH & MEDICINE ⚖ JUSTICE ✝ RELIGION ▯ SCIENCE

HENRY I

BORN 1068 • ACCEDED 1100 • DIED 1135

The circumstances of William II's death had always been regarded with suspicion, but because he was so disliked by lord and peasant alike little attempt was made to solve the mystery and his death was never avenged. Chief among the suspects was Henry, William I's youngest son, who was in the vicinity at the time and on hearing news of his brother's death seized the royal treasure at Winchester and rode straight to London to declare himself king.

UNFAITHFUL HUSBAND

Henry married Edith, the daughter of Malcolm III, king of Scotland, and so united the two countries. She used the name Matilda and they remained married for 18 years. Henry had several mistresses who bore him no less than 22 illegitimate children.

'LION OF JUSTICE'

Henry was a shrewd man who knew he had to placate the Saxon population to strengthen his position. On succeeding to the throne he promised good governance and introduced several legal reforms, including an improved judiciary.

CLAIM TO THE THRONE

The rightful heir to the English throne on William II's death was his son Robert, already Duke of Normandy. Henry, Robert's younger brother, seized the crown and proclaimed himself king three days later. On hearing the news Robert invaded England to claim the throne. After several attempts he eventually failed and was imprisoned by Henry , who then seized his lands in Normandy.

ROCHESTER CASTLE

Rochester Castle was first built in 1086 by Bishop Gundulph and guarded an important crossing of the main London to Dover road over the River Medway, in Kent. The magnificent keep was added in 1127, built by royal charter issued by Henry. It is the tallest keep in Europe and remains one of the most original Norman buildings still standing.

1100	daughter of	1101	Exchequer is founded.	Robert's lands
William's brother	Malcolm III, King	Robert of Normandy	1106	in Normandy.
becomes king	of Scotland.	invades England but is	War breaks out between	1110
as Henry I.	1100	repulsed by Henry.	Henry and Robert again.	Archbishop Anselm dies.
1100	Charter of	1101	Robert defeated and held	1110
Henry marries	Liberties issued.	Court of the	prisoner. Henry seizes	Pipe Rolls introduced.

🏛 ARCHITECTURE   📖 ARTS & LITERATURE   ⚑ EXPLORATION   💣 FAMOUS BATTLES

THE WHITE SHIP

The *'White Ship'*, reputedly the finest vessel of its day, ran aground and sank in the Channel in November 1120, while returning from Normandy. Henry's only legitimate son and heir, William, drowned in the accident caused, it is believed, by a drunken crew. His death left the crown without a male heir, resulting in years of civil war between King Stephen and Henry's daughter the Empress Matilda.

HEIR TO THE THRONE

The year after the 'White Ship' tragedy Henry married again, to Adela of Louvain, in the hope of producing another son, but the marriage was fruitless. Instead, Henry had to try and persuade his barons to accept his daughter Matilda as his heir.

UNTIMELY DEATH

Henry had long feared an assassination attempt and slept with his sword by his side. He died, it is believed from food poisoning, after eating infected lampreys (a sea-food) at Rouen, in France.

THE GREAT SEAL

This picture shows the great royal seal of Henry I. All of the medieval kings had their own, individual seal, usually depicting the monarch himself. Made of embossed metal it was used to seal all official letters and writs by pressing it firmly into hot wax. Only authorised people could break the seal and read the contents of the document.

⚕ LEPER HOSPITAL

St. Bartholomew's Hospital, in London, was founded in 1123 and is reputed to be the oldest hospital in England. Early medieval hospitals were mostly run by the Church and did not provide health care in the modern sense, but simply provided 'hospitality' in the form of food and lodging for the chronically sick, usually lepers, who could not look after themselves.

⚖ CHARTER OF LIBERTIES

Immediately he succeeded to the throne Henry issued a Charter of Liberties promising the people of England that he would govern well and fairly, treating Saxon and Norman equally.

⚖ PIPE ROLLS

Henry made sheriffs and other royal officials accountable by introducing the Pipe Rolls, which detailed all official expenditure. They remained in use until 1834.

1118
Henry's wife Matilda, dies.
1120
Henry's son and heir William dies in 'White
Ship' tragedy.
1121
Henry marries Adela of Louvain.
1123
St. Bartholomew's
Hospital founded in London.
1126
Henry persuades barons to accept Matilda, his daughter as queen,
on his death.
1135
Henry I dies of food poisoning at Rouen, in France.

📜 GOVERNMENT   ⚕ HEALTH & MEDICINE   ⚖ JUSTICE   ✝ RELIGION   ▯ SCIENCE

STEPHEN

BORN 1096 • ACCEDED 1135 • DIED 1154

& MATILDA

BORN 1102 • ACCEDED 1141 • DEPOSED 1141 • DIED 1167

Stephen had sworn his allegiance to Matilda as heir to the throne, along with most other barons, but when Henry I died he usurped the throne and had himself crowned king. Almost the entire duration of his reign was spent in civil war as the barons divided their allegiance between him and Matilda. Although a good-natured and courteous man, he was also weak. A state of anarchy developed in which the barons plundered the country at will while, it was said, 'Christ and His saints slept'.

SIEGE OF OXFORD

The turning point in the civil war came in 1142 when Stephen besieged Matilda in Oxford Castle. One night, after three months of stalemate, Matilda escaped in a white robe over the frozen river Isis. Shortly afterwards the garrison was starved into submission.

MATILDA FLEES

In 1145 Stephen won a resounding victory over Matilda at the Battle of Faringdon. Three years later she gave up the fight and left England for France.

RIVAL CLAIMANTS

When Henry I's only legitimate son, William, died in 1120 his daughter Matilda became heir to the throne. Henry spent the last years of his reign persuading the barons to swear allegiance to her. However, Henry's nephew Stephen, by his sister Adela, also claimed the throne on the grounds that as William I's eldest surviving grandson he was the rightful heir.

1135	1136	1138	at Battle of the Standard.	Lincoln, and is
Henry's nephew,	Civil war breaks	David I of Scotland	1139	then imprisoned at
Stephen, usurps	out between barons	invades England in support	Matilda returns to England	Bristol Castle.
the throne from	who support	of his niece, Matilda.	from France to claim throne.	Matilda rules for
Matilda, Henry's	either Stephen	1138	1141	just 6 months,
daughter.	or Matilda.	David I defeated by Stephen	Stephen captured at	but is not crowned.

🏛 ARCHITECTURE 📖 ARTS & LITERATURE 🏳 EXPLORATION 💣 FAMOUS BATTLES

ARUNDEL CASTLE

Arundel Castle, in Sussex, was begun in the late 11th century and was granted by Henry I to the Albini family. In 1139 William de Albini, who supported Matilda in the civil war, gave shelter to her. When Stephen arrived at the castle with his army to besiege it, Matilda fled to the West Country.

FAVERSHAM ABBEY

Stephen and his wife, also named Matilda, were buried at Faversham Abbey, in Kent, which he had founded some years earlier. The abbey was almost totally destroyed at the Dissolution and the royal tombs thrown into the nearby creek. A plaque in the church of St. Mary of Charity states that their bones were transferred there.

THE KING HELD PRISONER

In 1141 Matilda's supporters defeated Stephen at the Battle of Lincoln. He was taken prisoner and held at Bristol Castle, but was afterwards exchanged for Robert, Earl of Gloucester, Matilda's half-brother. During Stephen's confinement Matilda briefly declared herself queen for six months. Upon entering London Matilda upset the people of the city with her arrogance. They forced her to leave, preventing her from formally claiming the throne.

BATTLE OF THE STANDARD

Matilda's uncle, David I of Scotland, lent his support to her cause by invading the north of England in 1138, but he was defeated by Stephen's army at the Battle of the Standard at Northallerton, in Yorkshire.

TREATY OF WESTMINSTER

In 1153 Henry of Anjou, Matilda's son, took up the claim for the English throne where his mother had left off. Henry quickly gathered support and at the Treaty of Westminster it was agreed that Stephen should remain king until his death, but then the throne should pass to Henry and not to Stephen's heirs, bringing 19 years of civil war to an end.

MATILDA

Matilda was born in 1102 to Henry I and Edith of Scotland, also known as Matilda. She was arrogant, had a fiery temper and a quite objectionable nature that caused many of her allies to desert her. In 1129 she married Geoffrey Plantagenet, Count of Anjou. Their son ruled England as Henry II, so beginning a new royal dynasty, the Plantagenets.

1142 Matilda escapes from the siege of Oxford.
1145 Stephen defeats Matilda at the

Battle of Farringdon.
1148 Matilda concedes defeat and flees England for Anjou.
1151 Matilda's son, Henry,

succeeds his father Geoffrey, as Count of Anjou.
1153 Henry re-opens civil war with Stephen.

1153 Treaty of Westminster, Stephen agrees to pass throne to Henry Plantagenet on his death and not to his son William.

1154 Stephen dies and the throne passes to Matilda's son, Henry Plantagenet, who becomes king as Henry II.

GOVERNMENT HEALTH & MEDICINE JUSTICE RELIGION SCIENCE

HENRY II

BORN 1133 • ACCEDED 1154 • DIED 1189

INVASION OF IRELAND

In 1155 Pope Adrian IV (left) gave sanction to Henry to invade Ireland and bring its church under papal control. In 1166 Henry sent an army to Ireland, led by Richard de Clare, Earl of Pembroke, following an appeal by one of the Irish kings, Dermot MacMurrough, king of Leinster, to help him crush opposition by the other Irish chieftains. Five years later Henry invaded Ireland himself and soon earned homage from all the Irish kings and proclaimed himself Lord of Ireland. Later that year, at the Council of Cashel, Henry forced the Irish church to submit to papal authority.

LICENCE TO CRENELLATE

During the civil wars of Stephen's reign a state of anarchy existed and many barons erected castles unlawfully. One of Henry's first acts was to destroy all unlicensed, or adulterine castles and replace them with royal strongholds. Any baron who wanted to fortify his house had to seek a 'licence to crenellate' from the king.

DOVER CASTLE

Dover Castle, at the nearest point between England and France, stands high on the cliffs overlooking the town and is one of our finest medieval castles.

A great favourite of Henry's, he expended a great deal of money on its construction. The magnificent keep he built is one of the largest and most complex such structures ever built. It is surrounded by two tiers of concentric curtain walls, containing a fine array of towers and gatehouses.

*f*ollowing the turmoil of Stephen's reign, England needed a strong king to re-unite a divided nation. It found him in Henry II, the son of Matilda and Geoffrey Plantagenet. He came to the throne at just 21, a strong, robust and well-educated man. Despite a fiery temper, he was a fair man who ruled well and introduced many legal and church reforms.

THOMAS BECKET

Thomas Becket was born of humble parents in 1118. In about 1144 he entered service to Theobald, Archbishop of Canterbury. A well-educated man, Theobald recommended him to Henry II, who in 1154 appointed him Chancellor. Becket and Henry quickly became friends and he actively supported many of the king's reforms. When Henry made him archbishop in 1162 he expected Becket to continue with his support, but Becket took his new position seriously and opposed Henry's church reforms. They quarrelled and Becket was forced into exile in France between 1164-70.

THE MURDER OF BECKET

Threatened with excommunication, Henry allowed Becket to return to England in 1170, but the two soon quarrelled again. The king is said to have exclaimed aloud: 'Will no-one rid me of this turbulent priest?' Whereupon four of his knights set out for Canterbury and murdered Becket in his own cathedral on 29th December 1170. Three years later Becket was canonised.

1154	1155	*Henry leave to invade*	*Henry's church reforms.*	*Clarendon issued to limit*
Henry Plantagenet	*Thomas à Becket appointed*	*Ireland and bring the church*	**1164**	*power of Church. Leads*
becomes king	*Chancellor of England.*	*back under the rule of Rome.*	*Becket flees to*	*to conflict between*
of England as	**1155**	**1162**	*France in exile.*	*Henry and Becket.*
Henry II on	*Pope Adrian IV*	*Becket appointed Archbishop*	**1164**	**1166**
Stephen's death.	*issues papal 'bull' giving*	*of Canterbury to aid*	*Constitutions of*	*Assize of Clarendon*

🏛 **ARCHITECTURE**   📖 **ARTS & LITERATURE**   ⚑ **EXPLORATION**   ⬥ **FAMOUS BATTLES**

OXFORD UNIVERSITY FOUNDED

In 1168 English scholars, who had been studying at Paris, were expelled. They returned to England, settling at Oxford, which was already acquiring a name for itself as a centre of learning, and founded a university there.

In 1264 the first college, Merton, was founded. Several more quickly followed, establishing Oxford as the foremost university in Europe.

✝ CONSTITUTIONS OF CLARENDON

In January 1164 Henry issued the 'Constitutions of Clarendon', a set of 16 articles attempting to curb the power of the Church in England, which had grown considerably during the anarchy of Stephen's reign. Principal among them was Henry's claim that clerics who broke the law should be punished by secular courts and not have their punishments decided by the church, which formed the root of the quarrel with Becket.

⚖ ASSIZE OF CLARENDON

Clarendon Palace was one of Henry's favourite royal residences and he issued many writs from there, including the 'Assize of Clarendon', which introduced the idea of trial by jury for the first time. (Assizes were the periodic sessions by Westminster judges in county courts.)

REBELLIOUS FAMILY

In 1152 Henry married Eleanor of Aquitaine, but his family life was far from happy. Between 1173–4 his sons Henry, Geoffrey, Richard and John rebelled against him, encouraged by Eleanor. He put down the rebellion and kept Eleanor a virtual prisoner for the last 15 years of his reign.

THE KING'S PENANCE

Whether he was directly responsible or not for Becket's murder, Henry was certainly implicated and accepted a public penance for his martyrdom, which included flagellation by the monks of Christ Church, Canterbury. Becket's tomb at Canterbury became the most popular place of pilgrimage in England until Henry VIII dissolved the monasteries in 1536–40.

---

introduces trial by jury.
1166
First invasion force by England sent to Ireland in response to request by one of the Irish kings,

Dermot McMurrough.
1168
English scholars expelled from Paris, leads to foundation of Oxford University.

1170
Becket is murdered at Canterbury Cathedral.
1171
Henry II invades Ireland receives homage of

Irish kings and is accepted as Lord of Ireland.
1171
Council of Cashel makes Irish church acknowledge authority of Rome.

1173
Becket is canonised. Pilgrims begin visiting shrine at Canterbury.
1189
Henry dies in Anjou.

📜 GOVERNMENT   ⚗ HEALTH & MEDICINE   ⚖ JUSTICE   ✝ RELIGION   🧪 SCIENCE

RICHARD COEUR DE LION

Richard is usually depicted as a brave, warrior king, earning him the nickname 'Lionheart'. Although undoubtedly a competent soldier, he was also a very cruel man. After the fall of Acre he ordered 2,700 captured Muslims to be executed.

THE CRUSADES

The Crusades were a series of wars (nine in all) waged from 1095 to liberate the Holy Land from Islamic rule. Though all of the crusades failed in their objective, there was no shortage of volunteers, who might win remission for their sins by defeating the heathens.

A KING'S RANSOM

On his return from Palestine Richard was captured by Leopold, of Austria, and imprisoned by Henry VI, Emperor of Germany. A huge ransom was demanded for his safe return, which was raised in England, mostly through heavy taxation.

SALADIN

Saladin (Salah-ad-Din, 1138–93) was a Turkish leader of Kurdish descent who defeated the Fatimid dynasty in Egypt and declared himself Sultan. In 1187 he seized Jerusalem, which prompted the Third Crusade, when the combined forces of Western Christendom were sent against him. Although often depicted as a cruel man, he was in fact a very learned patron of the arts and sciences, much respected for his generosity and chivalry.

RICHARD I
BORN 1157 • ACCEDED 1189 • DIED 1199

Richard I was born on 8th September 1157 at Beaumont Palace in Oxford. The third and eldest surviving son of Henry II and Eleanor of Aquitaine, he succeeded to the throne in 1189. Richard spent barely seven months of his 10 year reign in this country, and three of those were in the first year of his accession. His queen, Berengaria of Navarre, never set foot in England. A powerfully-built man, he was also musical and well-educated, though he spoke little English. He used England merely as a source of revenue to finance his wars abroad.

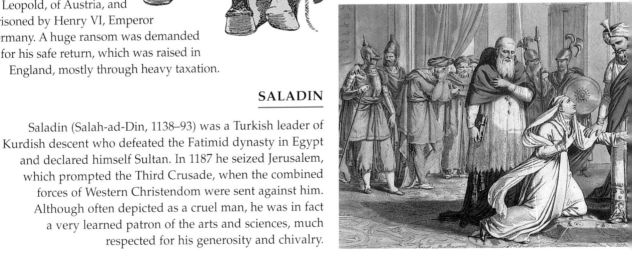

1189 Henry's eldest son becomes king as Richard I. **1189** Richard embarks upon	the Third Crusade to the Holy Land with Philip of France. **1189** William Longchamp appointed Chancellor to	govern England in Richard's absence. **1189** Scotland gains independence (surrendered to Henry II in 1173)	from Richard in return for cash payment to help finance his crusades to Holy Lands. **1191** Longchamp falls	from power and Prince John assumes government of the country during Richard's absence.

🏛 ARCHITECTURE   📖 ARTS & LITERATURE   ⚑ EXPLORATION   🔥 FAMOUS BATTLES

CHÂTEAU GAILLARD

Richard I supervised the building of Château Gaillard, in Normandy, overlooking the Seine at Les Andelys. Built in just two years (1196–98) it incorporated many sophisticated innovations, including concentric walls, rock-cut ditches and an elliptical citadel at the centre. It stood at the boundary between Richard's duchy in Normandy and the French king's lands. Once considered impregnable, it fell to Philip II of France in 1204.

A ROYAL PARDON

Following his return from captivity in 1194, Richard stayed in England only a few months before departing to protect his dominions in France. He was shot by a crossbow-man during the siege of Chalus-Chabrol. The wound turned gangrenous, but he forgave the bowman on his deathbed on 6th April 1199. He was buried at Fontevrault Abbey and was the last English monarch to be buried in France.

THE CRUSADES

The Third Crusade, led by Richard I, was the most successful. The crusaders suffered terribly in the heat, and from disease, especially dysentery. Richard took the city of Acre and reached an agreement with Saladin to allow Christians free passage to Jerusalem, but the holy city remained in Muslim hands until 1917.

ROBIN HOOD

In the popular legend of Robin Hood, a disinherited Saxon nobleman led a band of outlaws against the tyranny of John, Richard's brother (who ruled England in Richard's absence) robbing the rich to give to the oppressed poor. While his existence cannot be proved with any certainty, stories of his exploits were circulating as early as 1262.

1191
Richard captures city of Acre in the Holy Land and defeats Saladin at Arsouf.

1192
Richard makes agreement with Saladin to allow Christians to enter Jerusalem without fear of recriminations.

1192
Richard is captured on his return from Palestine by Duke of Austria who hands him over to Henry VI, Emperor of Germany.

Richard is held to ransom.
1194
Ransom paid and Richard is released.
1194
Richard returns to

England but leaves soon after to defend his lands in France.
1199
Richard is killed at Chalus, in France.

📖 GOVERNMENT   ⚗ HEALTH & MEDICINE   ⚖ JUSTICE   ✝ RELIGION   🏺 SCIENCE

JOHN

BORN 1166 • ACCEDED 1199 • DIED 1216

LOSS OF THE CROWN JEWELS

Shortly before his death John's entourage met with an accident in the treacherous marshes of the Wash. Several of his followers drowned and the royal chest, containing jewels and a great deal of money, was lost.

THE BARONS REBEL

The conflict between John and his barons had been building up over many years. High taxation, disputes with the church, the loss of the French domains and tampering with the legal system culminated in civil war, the barons claiming that John had abused his royal powers.

ohn's reign is overshadowed by one or two major events of the period, which belie the realities. He was an able administrator and a much better king than history has portrayed him. In truth, although he was implicated in a plot to usurp the crown from his brother, many of the problems he faced were in fact caused by Richard I, who had neglected England. The cost of the Third Crusade and Richard's ransom had to be met through high taxation. John inherited a near bankrupt country with many inherent problems, not least a very dissatisfied nobility.

1199 Richard's brother, John, becomes king.	France to Philip II. **1208** Pope Innocent III issues an Interdict against England, banning most church services.	**1209** John is excommunicated by the pope. **1212** Pope declares John is no longer the rightful	king of England. **1212** Children's Crusade, -ill-fated crusade by 30,000 children from France and Germany	to Holy Land. Most died or were sold into slavery. **1213** John gives in to pope's demands.
1204 John loses most of his lands in				

🏠 ARCHITECTURE   📖 ARTS & LITERATURE   🔎 EXPLORATION   💣 FAMOUS BATTLES

PRINCE OF PLEASURE

John was well-educated and quite fastidious. He liked to dress in fine clothes and take frequent baths. He enjoyed entertaining at court and had a passion for hunting.

'LACKLAND'

Although England accepted John as king, the barons in France regarded Arthur, John's nephew by his dead elder brother Geoffrey, to be the rightful heir to the Plantagenet empire. War broke out with France, which went disastrously for John. By 1204 he had lost virtually all his French lands, earning him the title 'John Lackland'.

EXCOMMUNICATION

John frequently quarrelled with the church, particularly over the pope's choice of Stephen Langton as Archbishop of Canterbury. He seized much of the church's property in England, an act for which he was excommunicated in 1209.

SUSPICIOUS DEATH

Following the tragedy of the Wash, John made his way to Newark Castle, in Nottinghamshire, one of the king's favourite residences. He is supposed to have caught a fever and died a few days later. The circumstances of his death were suspicious, but never investigated, because with his passing the civil war between the barons ended.

MAGNA CARTA

The barons turned to Stephen Langton, Archbishop of Canterbury, who helped them draw up the Great Charter. The original draft signed by John on 15th June 1215 contained 63 clauses outlining the rights and responsibilities of the crown and the nobles. The king was no longer allowed to govern at will, but only within the confines of the charter. Many of the clauses were specific to the barons and the rights of the church and had little effect on the lives of ordinary people, but it is now regarded as a milestone in our constitutional history. Several versions of the charter, with amendments, were drawn up, the last one signed by Henry III in 1225.

✠ INTERDICT

In 1208 John incurred the wrath of the pope, Innocent III, who responded by issuing an Interdict against England. All church services were banned, with the exception of baptisms and funerals.

● SIEGE OF ROCHESTER CASTLE

In October 1215 rebellious barons seized the royal castle at Rochester, in Kent. John, seldom given due credit for his military prowess, personally supervised siege operations to retake it. His miners and sappers succeeded in bringing down the south-east corner of the keep, a remarkable achievement. The garrison capitulated after just six weeks.

1214	discuss terms of	Magna Carta	1216	to help in civil
French defeat John at	Magna Carta.	at Runneymede.	John loses his personal	war with John.
Battle of Bouvines.	1215	1215	possessions in the Wash.	1216
1214	John reluctantly	Pope allows John	1216	John dies at
English barons meet at	agrees to barons'	to ignore Magna Carta;	Barons invite	Newark castle
Bury St. Edmunds to	demands and signs	civil war ensues.	French Prince, Louis,	(foul-play is suspected).

📜 GOVERNMENT   ⚗ HEALTH & MEDICINE   ⚖ JUSTICE   ✠ RELIGION   📖 SCIENCE

HENRY III

BORN 1207 • ACCEDED 1216 • DIED 1272

Henry was only nine years old when his father, John, died in 1216. John, perhaps anticipating his demise, had already made provisions for a regent to rule during Henry's minority. After 1227 Henry took control of the government, but years of misrule eventually led to civil war again, this time resulting in the formation of a parliament. Despite these problems, Henry's was a long reign, marked by many advancements in architecture and the arts.

HENRY'S RELATIONSHIP WITH HIS BARONS

The growth of Parliament occurred during Henry III's reign, largely because of his embittered relationship with his barons, inherited from his father, King John. The situation was made worse after his marriage to Eleanor of Provence in 1236 when he gave several French noblemen influential positions of power at court.

THE 'DAUPHIN' OF FRANCE

During the civil war of John's reign the rebel barons had invited the French prince, Louis, to take the throne of England. Following John's death, many barons withdrew their support in favour of Henry. Louis was finally defeated at Lincoln in 1217 and returned to France.

SIMON DE MONTFORT

Known as the 'father of English Parliament', Simon de Montfort was leader of the rebel barons in the ongoing civil war with the king. Although parliaments, or councils, had been known since Saxon times, de Montfort was determined to make government more accountable and open to all classes, and not reliant on the whims of the ruling monarch. He defeated Henry at Lewes in 1264 and called the first open English Parliament the following year.

THE REGENCY

Between 1216-27 England was ruled by two regents, William the Marshal, Earl of Pembroke, and Hubert de Burgh, two very capable administrators. William died in 1219 and when Henry took control in 1227 he retained Hubert de Burgh as his adviser.

1216 *Henry III becomes king at just nine years old.*	**1217** *Treaty of Lambeth creates peace between England and France and between the king and his barons.*	**1219** *William the Marshal dies. Hubert de Burgh rules alone.*	*down attempt by Louis VIII of France to seize English throne.*	**1233/4** *Rebellion against the king led by Richard Marshal, Earl of Pembroke defeated.*
1217 *A French attempt to seize the English throne fails.*		**1222** *Hubert de Burgh puts*	**1227** *Henry assumes control of government.*	**1238** *Simon de Montfort*

AGE OF LEARNING

Although not the ablest of political leaders, Henry was a great patron of the arts. During his reign the universities of Oxford and Cambridge both flourished.

KENILWORTH CASTLE

Kenilworth Castle, in Warwickshire, was first built about 1120 by Geoffrey de Clinton and was later granted to Simon de Montfort. He used it as his base during the civil war with Henry III. By Tudor times the castle had assumed palatial proportions and was one of the finest residences in the country. The castle afterwards passed to the Earls of Leicester. Elizabeth I stayed there with Lord Dudley for 19 days during one of her royal progresses.

PROVISIONS OF OXFORD

At a meeting of parliament in Oxford in 1258 the rebel barons forced Henry to sign a series of documents which effectively limited absolute royal power. Henry rebuked the 'provisions' in 1261 and ignored them altogether after de Montfort's death in 1265.

THE FIRST ENGLISH PARLIAMENT

Although the idea of a parliament, where the views of people from different factions could be heard, had been in existence for several centuries, it carried few constitutional rights. Parliament usually consisted of a handful of the king's trusted allies and acted mostly in an advisory capacity. The parliament called by Simon de Montfort in 1265 is regarded as a milestone in constitutional history because, for the first time, it took the views of all social groups, except peasants, into account.

BATTLE OF EVESHAM

Some of the rebel barons decided to leave Simon de Montfort to take the king's side in the civil war. Henry's son, Edward, defeated de Montfort at the Battle of Evesham in 1265. Although the seeds of parliamentary government had been sown, Henry resumed control of the country for the remainder of his reign.

marries Henry's sister, Eleanor.
1258
Simon de Montfort leads revolt against Henry's misgovernment.

1258
Provisions of Oxford, limits royal power.
1261
Henry refuses to acknowledge the Provisions

of Oxford, which leads to further baronial revolt.
1264
Baron's war breaks out, Henry defeated by de Montfort.

1265
Simon de Montfort summons the first English Parliament.
1265
Simon de Montfort

killed at the Battle of Evesham.
1272
Henry III dies at Westminster.

GOVERNMENT   HEALTH & MEDICINE   JUSTICE   RELIGION   SCIENCE

📜 MODEL PARLIAMENT

Following on from the political reforms of his father's reign, Edward is credited with calling the first democratically elected parliament (at least partially) known as the 'Model Parliament', which comprised lords, clergy, knights and elected representatives from the shires and towns.

⚖️ STATUTE OF WINCHESTER

The first Justices of the Peace were introduced as a result of the 'Statute of Winchester' in 1285, along with controls against highway robbery and the right for local communities to police themselves against violent attacks.

🔥 BATTLE OF STIRLING BRIDGE

The Scots rose against Edward in 1297 under the leadership of William Wallace, who defeated Edward at the Battle of Stirling Bridge.

🔥 BATTLE OF FALKIRK

Edward turned the tables on Wallace in 1298 when he defeated him at the Battle of Falkirk. Wallace continued to lead Scottish resistance against the English until his arrest and execution in 1305, after which Robert Bruce led the revolt against Edward.

CAERNARFON CASTLE

Caernarfon Castle was begun in 1282 and from the start was meant to impress the newly conquered Welsh as his new capital. The high walls, incorporating several massive towers and gatehouses, are constructed of coloured bands of masonry, purposely mimicking the walls of Constantinople. The internal lodgings were never completed and it remains virtually intact today, one of the finest medieval castles ever built.

CONQUEST OF WALES

Edward launched his conquest of Wales in 1277. Much of southern and mid-Wales quickly submitted to his rule, but the people of north Wales held out from their mountain retreats in Snowdonia until 1284. Edward built a ring of mighty castles and established walled towns with English settlements to subjugate them. In 1301 he declared his son, Edward, to be the Prince of Wales, a title still held by the ruling monarch's eldest son.

PRINCE LLWELYN

The last independent Prince of Wales, Llwelyn Yr Ail, refused to acknowledge Edward as overlord of Wales and led several rebellions against him from his Snowdonia stronghold. He was overcome and killed at Builth in 1282. Two years later all of Wales finally subjected to Edward.

1272
Edward I becomes king whilst on Crusade to the Holy Land.
1274
Edward I returns to England and is crowned king.

1277
Edward invades North Wales in an attempt to force Prince Llwelyn to pay homage.
1279
Statute of Mortmain issued

to stop land being given to the church to avoid taxes.
1282
Edward invades North Wales again and defeats Prince Llwelyn.

1284
Statute of Rhuddlan ends Welsh independence.
1285
Statute of Winchester controls highway robbery and

introduces Justices of the Peace.
1290
Edward expels Jews from England.
1292
Edward elects John Balliol to

🏛️ ARCHITECTURE　　📖 ARTS & LITERATURE　　🏴 EXPLORATION　　🔥 FAMOUS BATTLES

EDWARD I

BORN 1239 • ACCEDED 1272 • DIED 1307

Edward was away on the 8th Crusade to the Holy Land, with his uncle Louis IX of France, when he heard of his father's death. Louis died of plague in 1270 but Edward continued to Acre only to find the allied leaders in disarray. The crusade failed and Edward returned home to be crowned king, in August 1274. He was a formidable soldier who spent much of his reign trying to unite England, Scotland and Wales into one kingdom, with partial success. He was also a very able and just ruler, responsible for many political and social reforms.

'LONGSHANKS'

Edward was over 6 ft. tall, when the average height was about 5 ft. 4 ins., earning him the title 'longshanks'. An athletic, robust man, with jet black hair, he was considered handsome, though he is believed to have had a slight speech impediment.

ELEANOR OF CASTILE

Edward married Eleanor of Castile in 1154 and together they had 16 children. He was devoted to her and was heartbroken when she died. When her body was carried from Nottinghamshire to Westminster he had a memorial cross erected at each of the 12 resting places, including Charing Cross, in London.

'HAMMER OF THE SCOTS'

Although Edward earned the nickname 'Hammer of the Scots', he never fully conquered Scotland. In 1292 he was asked to mediate in choosing the Scottish heir and chose John Balliol, a weak man who paid homage to Edward. When Balliol rebelled against him Edward invaded Scotland and declared himself king. The Scots refused to accept him and Edward died in 1307 on his third attempt to conquer Scotland.

JEWS EXPELLED

In 1290 Edward instigated the first banishment of the Jews, more on political and financial grounds than as religious persecution. He seized all their property and any debts still owed to them.

STONE OF SCONE

The kings of Scotland had for centuries been crowned at Scone Abbey. The ceremonial coronation stone (a large, rectangular boulder believed to date from prehistoric times) was seized by Edward I in 1296 when he declared himself king of Scotland. It was taken to Westminster Abbey and placed beneath the coronation throne, where it stayed until 1996, when it was returned to Scotland, not to Scone, which is now ruinous, but to Edinburgh Castle.

become king of Scotland.
1295
Model Parliament is summoned.
1296
Edward invades Scotland.

1296
Edward deposes Balliol and declares himself king of Scotland.
Removes Stone of Scone to London.

1297
William Wallace defeats Edward at Battle of Stirling Bridge.
1298
Edward invades Scotland

again, defeats Wallace.
1301
Edward's eldest son created Prince of Wales.
1305
William Wallace executed.

1306
Robert Bruce becomes king of Scotland.
1307
Edward dies en-route to re-invade Scotland.

GOVERNMENT   HEALTH & MEDICINE   JUSTICE   RELIGION   SCIENCE

EDWARD II

BORN 1284 • ACCEDED 1307 • DEPOSED 1307 • DIED 1327

dward II was the fourth, but eldest surviving son of Edward I. His reign is best remembered for its lack of military campaigning, unlike his father's, and also for the gruesome circumstances surrounding his death. Although often dismissed as an inept administrator, England actually prospered during his rule, due in no small part to low taxation; his father had raised taxes considerably to pay for his wars in Wales and Scotland.

THE KING IS MURDERED

Following his dispossession, Edward was held prisoner in Kenilworth Castle, where he formally abdicated the throne. He was then imprisoned at Berkeley Castle, Gloucestershire, for six months. On the instructions of Isabella, Edward was murdered by the insertion of a red-hot poker into his rectum - a punishment normally reserved for homosexuals. The story goes that the king's screams could be heard outside the castle.

PIERS GAVESTON

Edward had little interest in government and entrusted much of the day-to-day work to a few ill-chosen but trusted advisers. One of these, Piers Gaveston, angered the barons because of his mismanagement. In 1312 he was captured and murdered by the king's enemies.

ISABELLA OF FRANCE

Edward married Isabella of France in 1308 and she bore him four children, but it was a loveless marriage. She openly had an affair with her lover, Roger Mortimer, and in 1326 they led a rebellion against the king, forcing his deposition in favour of his son.

1307
Edward, Prince of Wales accedes to the throne as Edward II.
1308
King's favourite, Piers Gaveston,

exiled for mismanagement of state affairs.
1309
Gaveston returns from exile.
1310
Edward's cousin Thomas,

🏛 ARCHITECTURE   📖 ARTS & LITERATURE   🗺 EXPLORATION   🔥 FAMOUS BATTLES

BATTLE OF BANNOCKBURN

Robert Bruce finally crushed the English at the Battle of Bannockburn in 1314, near Stirling Castle, and proclaimed himself king of Scotland.

THE DESPENSERS

Sir Hugh Despenser and his son, also Hugh, were two more of Edward's ill-chosen advisers who incurred the wrath of his opponents because of their mishandling of government. They were both cruelly murdered by Isabella in 1326. Hugh, the younger, was also accused of having a homosexual relationship with the king and was executed by being hanged, drawn, quartered and beheaded (shown left).

BARONS' REBELLION

Edward handed over the running of the country to a handful of favourites, who the barons felt had misgoverned the country. In 1310 they established a committee to try to control the hapless monarch, but to no avail. In 1322 they openly rebelled, led by Thomas, Earl of Lancaster, but the rebellion was defeated. The king was eventually deposed in 1327.

PRINCE OF WALES

Unfortunately, the popular tradition of the infant Edward being held aloft by Edward I in 1284 and presented to the Welsh as a prince, born in Wales but speaking no English, has little basis in fact. Edward was not created Prince of Wales until 1301.

The story was probably English propaganda put about by the Tudors in the 16th century to prove their Welsh ancestry.

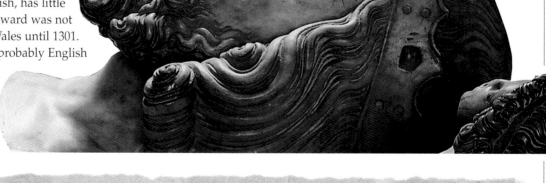

Earl of Lancaster, assumes control of government. **1310** Parliament installs Lords Ordainers	to curtail king's powers. **1312** Gaveston captured by king's enemies and executed.	**1314** English defeated by Robert Bruce at the Battle of Bannockburn. **1322** Baron's rebellion, led by	Thomas, Earl of Lancaster, defeated at Battle of Boroughbridge. **1326** Edward's wife, Isabella, leaves him for her lover.	**1327** Edward is formally deposed by Parliament. **1327** Edward is murdered in Berkeley castle.

🛒 GOVERNMENT   ⚕ HEALTH & MEDICINE   ⚖ JUSTICE   ✝ RELIGION   SCIENCE

EDWARD III

BORN 1312 • ACCEDED 1327 • DIED 1377

ORDER OF THE GARTER

Edward was the epitome of the medieval, chivalrous king. In 1348 he founded the Order of the Garter, a Chivalric order of knights, based at Windsor Castle, who took their inspiration directly from the epic tales of King Arthur's Knights of the Round Table. In keeping with this general theme, it was during Edward's reign that St. George was proclaimed patron saint of England.

dward came to the throne at the age of 14 in 1327. For the first three years of his reign the country was governed by his mother, Isabella, and her lover, Roger Mortimer. In 1330 Edward seized power for himself and set about righting some of the wrongs that had been directed towards his father. He removed Isabella from office and retired her with a pension, while Mortimer was tried and executed for his crimes. Edward was an heroic figure, like his grandfather, popular with the people because of his just government and victories over France. He was devoted to his wife, Philippa of Hainault, until her death in 1369. He named his new castle and township on the Isle of Sheppey in Kent, Queenborough, in her honour. Edward died eight years after Philippa, it is believed from senile dementia.

THE BLACK PRINCE

Edward III's eldest son, also Edward and known as the Black Prince because of the colour of his armour, died the year before his father in 1376 at the age of 46. He won his spurs at the Battle of Crecy in 1346 when just 16 years old and soon became the most feared warrior in Europe. A magnificent effigy of the prince can be seen above his tomb in Canterbury Cathedral.

1327 Edward III becomes king when his father is deposed. **1332** Parliament divided into two separate houses -	Lords and Commons. **1337** Start of '100 Years' War' with France. **1337** Edward claims the	French throne. **1340** Edward defeats French navy at Battle of Sluys. **1346** David II of Scotland	invades England but is defeated at Nevilles's Cross and held prisoner. **1346** French defeated at	Battle of Crécy. **1348** Edward founds chivalric Order of the Garter. **1349/50** Outbreak of Bubonic

🏛 ARCHITECTURE   📖 ARTS & LITERATURE   🗺 EXPLORATION   🔥 FAMOUS BATTLES

100 YEARS' WAR

Edward claimed the throne of France through his French mother, Isabella, marking the beginning of the 100 Years' War with France. The wars consisted of a series of battles during the period 1337-1453. The English had several early successes, but gradually the tide of the wars changed, with the French finally evicting the English in 1453 at the Battle of Châtillon.

LEGAL REFORMS

Some of the many legal reforms introduced by Edward were the right of Parliament to sanction all tax increases and the Statute of Treason, which for the first time laid down a legal definition as to what did or did not constitute treason.

WINDSOR CASTLE

Edward was born at Windsor Castle, Berkshire, in 1312. The first castle here was of the motte and bailey type and although substantially rebuilt since then it still preserves the typical hour-glass shape of such a castle with its central mound and two courtyards. Edward III transformed the castle into a royal palace from 1346 on. Subsequent monarchs have continued to embellish the buildings which, at nearly 13 acres in extent, form the largest residential castle in the world.

THE BLACK DEATH

The plague, known as the Black Death, is believed to have spread to England sometime in the mid-14th century from the Middle East, though similar diseases may have been around since Saxon times. There were several outbreaks and death was usually swift. Between ⅓ and ⅕ of the population is believed to have died in the 14th century alone. If a similar event occurred in Britain today, with the same ratio of deaths, nearly 20 million people would die.

PARLIAMENT DIVIDED

Edward's military achievements have sometimes eclipsed his prowess as an able and just administrator. He introduced several parliamentary reforms. In 1322 Parliament was divided into two houses, the Lords and the Commons, the former mostly hereditary, the latter elected - much as it is today. This was followed in 1362 by the replacement of French with English as the official language in courts and in parliament.

BATTLE OF CRECY

The Battle of Crecy, near the Somme, was the first major land battle of the 100 Years' War, where a small force of 10,000 English, many of them archers, won a resounding victory over the French. Edward oversaw the battle from a windmill, situated on a nearby hill.

Plague (the 'Black Death') decimates the English population.
1351
Statute of Labourers fixes prices and wages.
1352
Statute of Treason defines exact nature of treasonable offences.
1356
Black Prince defeats French at Battle of Poitiers.
1357
David of Scotland released from prison.
1362
English re-introduced as official language in courts and Parliament, instead of French.
1376
Death of Edward's son, and heir, the Black Prince.
1377
Edward III dies.

🏛 GOVERNMENT   🥄 HEALTH & MEDICINE   ⚖ JUSTICE   ✝ RELIGION   📄 SCIENCE

RICHARD II

BORN 1367 • ACCEDED 1377 • DEPOSED 1399 • DIED 1400

PEASANTS' REVOLT

The Peasants' Revolt of 1381 was a landmark in English social history, which might have led to open revolution. It was sparked off by the introduction of a poll tax in 1380, levied on individuals equally by the crown, regardless of ability to pay and not related to individual wealth. There were other causes too, in particular the 'Statute of Labourers', which restricted wages and working practices. The 14 year old king faced the rebels and agreed to their demands, but he later reneged on his word and many of the rebels were executed.

WAT TYLER

There were several ringleaders among those involved in the Peasants' Revolt, notably Jack Straw, John Ball and Wat Tyler. Many of the rebels disbanded after meeting Richard, but Tyler led an attack on the Tower of London and killed Simon Sudbury, Archbishop of Canterbury. At a second meeting with the king Tyler was killed by William Walworth, mayor of London.

ichard (the grandson of Edward III) came to the throne at something of a disadvantage. He was a 10 year old boy whose father (the Black Prince) had been a popular hero and he was destined, perhaps, to be ever in his shadow. Until 1389 the country was ruled by advisers. During this time there were several periods of social unrest. Although he ruled well for a while, Richard, a sickly man, was more interested in art and music than government and he became something of a tyrant in later years. He died in prison at just 33 years of age.

CLAIMS TO THE THRONE

Richard II was the son of Edward the Black Prince. Had his father lived he would probably have succeeded to the throne anyway, but when his grandfather Edward III died in 1377 there were those who thought the throne should pass to one of his other sons, John of Gaunt. John's son and Richard's cousin - Henry Bolingbroke - likewise had a strong claim to the throne, which he exercised when Richard proved incompetent to rule in 1399.

THE KING ABDICATES

Henry Bolingbroke returned from exile in 1399 to reclaim his inheritance. By then Richard, who had been behaving irrationally since the death of his first wife Anne in 1394, had incurred the wrath of his barons. Bolingbroke forced him to abdicate on the grounds of his misrule and imprisoned the king in Pontefract Castle, where he died, suspiciously, a few months later in 1400.

1377 Richard II succeeds his grandfather, Edward III, as king. **1377** Richard's uncles, John of	Gaunt and Thomas of Gloucester, rule England as regents. **1380** John Wycliffe translates New Testament into English.	**1381** Poll Tax introduced, leads to Peasants' Revolt. **1382** Richard marries Anne of Bohemia.	**1387** Lords Appellant take control of government. **1388** Scottish defeat English at Battle of Otterburn in	English borderlands. **1389** Richard resumes control of government. **1390** Robert II of

🏛 ARCHITECTURE   📖 ARTS & LITERATURE   ✒ EXPLORATION   🔥 FAMOUS BATTLES

HENRY YEVELE

Henry Yevele was a master mason and director of the king's works, responsible for designing many royal buildings, such as Westminster Hall. He was the architect entrusted by William of Wykeham (Chancellor and Bishop of Winchester) to rebuild the naves of Westminster Abbey and Canterbury Cathedral. He also designed the revolutionary circular castle at Queenborough, in Kent, which is believed to be the first castle built specifically for the use of firearms.

JOHN OF GAUNT

John of Gaunt (or Ghent, where he was born) was the fourth son of Edward III and accompanied his brother, the Black Prince, on many of his military campaigns. He became the Duke of Lancaster in 1362 and was very influential at court. He acted as mediator between his nephew, Richard II, and his discontented barons. Relations with the king became strained, however, and Richard exiled John's son, Henry Bolingbroke (later Henry IV) in 1399, when John died, and seized his possessions.

📖 GEOFFREY CHAUCER

Born about 1340, Geoffrey Chaucer earned his living as a soldier, courtier, civil servant and official poet to the court. He became Controller of Customs in London until 1386 and on a diplomatic journey through Italy in 1372 he became familiar with the works of Dante, which influenced his style of writing. His most celebrated work was 'The Canterbury Tales', a narrative story following the journeyings of a group of pilgrims, written sometime between 1387 and his death in 1400.

✟ THE BIBLE TRANSLATED

John Wycliffe was a master of Balliol College, Oxford, where he taught theology and spread his controversial views on church reform. His followers were known as Lollards. He was twice tried for heresy, unsuccessfully, but in 1382 he was finally condemned as a heretic. He escaped execution and retired to Lutterworth (where he translated the Bible into English), until his death in 1384.

📜 GOVERNMENT ⚕ HEALTH & MEDICINE ⚖ JUSTICE ✟ RELIGION 📄 SCIENCE

HENRY IV

BORN 1367 • ACCEDED 1399 • DIED 1413

FAMILY REVOLT

Although Henry was welcomed to the throne in 1399 there were many who challenged his authority. Following a mild stroke in 1405 the king's younger son, Thomas, set up a council with Thomas Arundel, Archbishop of Canterbury, to rival the king's court. They were gradually eased out of power by Henry's elder son and heir, Henry of Monmouth, who assumed many of the roles of government during the king's frequent bouts of illness.

OWAIN GLYNDWR

Under the leadership of Owain Glyndwr, who claimed to be descended from the last independent Prince of Wales, the Welsh rose in revolt against English rule, with help from the French.
The revolt began in 1401 and continued throughout Henry's reign. Independent Welsh parliaments were set up in 1404 and again in 1405 at the newly captured Harlech Castle. Unable to subdue the Welsh, the revolt only subsided following the death of Glyndwr in 1416, three years after the death of Henry.

enry Bolingbroke came to the English throne by forcing his cousin, Richard II, to abdicate and usurping the crown. In the ongoing dispute between the two, Richard had, in 1397, exiled Henry to France and seized his lands. Two years later Henry returned to reclaim his estates, expecting to have to do so by force, but was instead asked by Parliament to make a bid for the throne. He claimed the crown on the grounds that his father, John of Gaunt, was the fourth son of Edward III. Richard died in prison in Pontefract Castle in 1400.

HARLECH CASTLE

Begun by Edward I in 1283 during his Welsh campaigns of 1277-84, Harlech Castle was not finished until 1290. It stands on a lofty crag guarding the south-west approaches of Snowdonia and used to be much closer to the sea before land drainage left it some distance inland. It was captured from the English by Owain Glyndwr in 1404 and remains virtually complete today.

THE KING REPENTS

Henry is buried in a magnificent tomb in Canterbury. Shortly before he died, he begged forgiveness for usurping the crown from his cousin, Richard II.

1399
Richard II is deposed and imprisoned.
1399
Henry Bolinbroke returns from exile and claims throne.

Henry proclaims himself king and is crowned as Henry IV.
1400
The deposed king, Richard II dies at Pontefract Castle, it

is claimed through self-imposed starvation.
1400
The poet, Geoffrey Chaucer, dies shortly after completing 'The Canterbury Tales'.

1401
Start of Welsh revolt against English rule by Owain Glyndwr.
1402
State visit by Manuel II,

Byzantine emperor.
1403
Percy family, Dukes of Northumberland, revolt against Henry IV.

🏛 ARCHITECTURE   📖 ARTS & LITERATURE   ✒ EXPLORATION   ⚔ FAMOUS BATTLES

TEUTONIC KNIGHT

As a young man Henry travelled widely, throughout Europe and the Middle East, fighting alongside the Teutonic Knights, an order of religious knights who fought in the crusades, in Lithuania. He made a pilgrimage to Jerusalem and promised to return on a crusade himself, though he never did.

⚕ A HORRIBLE DEATH

Henry is believed to have contracted leprosy, or a similar debilitating disease, in 1406. Plagued by constant illness, he died of a seizure in 1413 aged just 46. A prophecy had foretold that he would die in Jerusalem. In fact, he died in the Jerusalem Chapel in Westminster Abbey.

● BATTLE OF SHREWSBURY

Henry's reign was plagued by rebellions. Most notable of these was the revolt led by his once loyal supporters, the Percys, Dukes of Northumberland. On 21st July 1403 Henry Percy, known as Harry Hotspur, was defeated at the Battle of Shrewsbury.

LONDON'S GUILDHALL

Guilds were professional or craft associations formed by merchants and traders in medieval towns to protect their mutual interests. They built magnificent guildhalls from where they conducted their business, which also often became the centres of local government. Probably the finest guildhall was built in London between 1411–26.

JOAN OF NAVARRE

Henry married Mary de Bohun in 1380, who bore him seven children, including the future king, Henry V. Following her death he married Joan of Navarre, in 1403, whose effigy can be seen above their canopied tomb in Canterbury Cathedral. Navarre was an independent kingdom on the French and Spanish borders.

EMPEROR MANUEL II

In 1402 Henry received Manuel II, the Byzantine emperor, at court on a state visit to England. The Byzantine empire grew out of what was the Eastern Roman Empire when that collapsed in the 5th century. Occupying much of what is now known as the Middle East, Byzantium resisted invasion from the feudal states of Europe until the early 14th century, when it fell to the Ottoman Turks.

1403 *Percy rebels defeated by Henry at Battle of Shrewsbury.*	*up independent Welsh Parliament.*	**1405** *Second Percy rebellion.*	**1406** *Henry IV contracts leprosy.*
1404 *Owain Glyndwr sets*	**1404** *Welsh form allegiance with French against English.*	**1405** *French send an army to help Welsh revolt against English.*	**1408** *Third Percy rebellion.* **1413** *Henry IV dies.*

📜 GOVERNMENT   ⚕ HEALTH & MEDICINE   ⚖ JUSTICE   ✝ RELIGION   ▯ SCIENCE

MONMOUTH CASTLE

Monmouth Castle was first built between 1067–71 during the Norman invasion of Wales and greatly extended later, principally during the reign of Edward I, when a fortified bridge and town wall were added. The castle was the birthplace, in 1387, of Henry V.

THE CAMBRIDGE PLOT

In 1415, a plot was uncovered to remove Henry from the throne in favour of his cousin Edmund Mortimer who, as Richard II's heir, had a stronger claim to the crown. Known as the Cambridge Plot, it was unsuccessful and the ringleaders were brought to trial for treason.

HENRY V

BORN 1387 • ACCEDED 1413 • DIED 1422

One of the first acts by Henry on becoming king in 1413, at the age of 25, was to renew Edward III's claim to the French throne. The war with France that followed served the dual purpose of extending his military prowess and in unifying a divided nobility against a common enemy. A zealous and religious man, Henry was also a scholar and a patron of the arts, who might have gone down in history as one of our greatest monarchs but for his untimely and premature death at the age of 35.

PREMATURE DEATH

Always a healthy, robust young man, Henry died somewhat prematurely during his French campaigns. He contracted dysentery and died at Vincennes Castle on 1st September 1422. Had he lived just a few weeks longer he would have inherited the French throne, for Charles VI followed him to the grave less than two months later. Henry is shown here being married to Katherine of France, Charles' sister.

R: DE: FRANCE·   ·h: LE: CINQVIESHE·

THE BATTLE OF AGINCOURT

One of the greatest and best remembered battles of the Middle Ages was fought at Agincourt (left), in France, during the 100 Years' War. On 25th October 1415 Henry led an English force of just 9,000 men, one-third the size of the opposing French army. The French relied on cavalry, but they became bogged down in heavy mud and fell to the mercy of the English archers. About 7000 Frenchmen lost their lives, compared to just 400 English.

SHAKESPEARE'S HERO

The popular image of Henry V as a saintly hero king is largely an invention of Shakespeare. The Tudor monarchs were descended from the House of Lancaster and it suited their purpose to make heroes of their ancestors. While unquestionably a brave and able soldier, many contemporary chroniclers portray him as arrogant and manipulative.

HEIR TO THE FRENCH THRONE

At the 'Treaty of Troyes', in 1420, Henry forced the French king, Charles VI (considered by many to be mad), to make him his heir and regent of France. He also requested the hand of Charles's daughter, Katherine, in marriage. They were married later the same year, thus briefly uniting the crowns of England and France.

WELSH REVOLT

The Welsh revolt against English rule, led by Owain Glyndwr, was largely dealt with by Henry, as Prince of Wales, during his father's reign, though he never succeeded in finally defeating the Welsh. The revolt diffused itself on the death of Glyndwr in 1416, but the young Henry cut his military teeth on the Welsh campaigns and learned the art of tactics against superior odds.

WAR WITH FRANCE

A brilliant soldier and tactician, Henry took advantage of the weakened state of the French monarchy, damaged by corrupt government and civil war. He won several resounding victories and recaptured Normandy and parts of Aquitaine. The victories were largely made possible by the skill of the English archers. If captured, the French cut off their fore and middle fingers to prevent them from drawing bows again. Before battle it became the practice for archers to wave their two fingers in a V-sign as a gesture of defiance, a derisive gesture still used today.

1413
Henry V succeeds his father to the throne.
1415
The Cambridge Plot (an attempt to depose Henry and
replace him with his cousin, Edmund Mortimer, Earl of March) is put down by Henry.
1415
Henry declares war on
France and makes claim for French throne.
1415
English defeat French at the Battle of Agincourt, against massive odds.
1420
Treaty of Troyes; Henry becomes Regent of France and heir to French throne.
1420
Henry marries Katherine,
daughter of Charles VI of France.
1422
Henry V dies of dysentery in France just 2 months before succeeding to the French throne.

📜 GOVERNMENT   ⚕ HEALTH & MEDICINE   ⚖ JUSTICE   ✝ RELIGION   📋 SCIENCE

BOY KING

Henry was just 10 months old when he succeeded first, to the English throne on the death of his father in 1422, and then to the French throne on the death of his grandfather, Charles VI, two months later. During his minority Humphrey, Duke of Gloucester, was appointed Regent of England and John, Duke of Bedford, Regent of France. Henry took over governance himself at the age of 15 in 1437.

HENRY VI

**BORN 1421 • ACCEDED 1422 • DEPOSED 1461
RESTORED 1470 • DEPOSED 1471 • DIED 1471**

n less warlike times Henry VI might have become one of our better kings, but he was ill-equipped to deal with the violence and bitter political quarrels of his time. A gentle, well-educated and devoutly religious man, he had a naive, almost unworldly nature. This simplicity was seen as weakness by his enemies, who ruthlessly exploited him. His reign was plagued by civil war, eventually resulting in his deposition and murder in 1471 at the age of 49.

MENTAL ILLNESS

Throughout his life Henry suffered from recurring bouts of mental illness, inherited from his maternal grandfather. The first attack came at the age of 32, in 1454, and his cousin Richard, Duke of York, was made Protector of England during his incapacitation.

JOAN OF ARC
(1412–31)

Born to a peasant family in Domrémy, France, Joan of Arc began (in 1429) the revolt against Henry VI that eventually led to the expulsion of the English from France, claiming her inspiration in a vision from God. Captured by the English in 1431 she was burned at the stake in Rouen, though the French continued the fight in her name. In 1920 she was canonised by Pope Benedict XV.

1422
Henry VI succeeds his father to the throne.
1422
Henry VI becomes king of France on the death
of his grandfather.
1422
During Henry's minority, John, Duke of Bedford, appointed Regent of

PATRON OF LEARNING

Henry was a quiet, learned man, who encouraged others to study by founding the King's College of Our Lady at Eton (left) in 1440. The following year he founded King's College at Cambridge University to receive its scholars.

WARS OF THE ROSES

In 1455 Richard, Duke of York, who had been instated as Protector during Henry's mental illness, was dismissed. He rebelled against Henry and assumed control of the government, marking the beginning of the 'Wars of the Roses' (see pages 14-15), a dynastic struggle for the English throne.

END OF THE 100 YEARS' WAR

The 100 Years' War with France, begun in 1337 by Edward III when asserting his claim to the French throne, came to an end in 1453 when the English were finally driven out of France. All of England's possessions in France, with the exception of Calais, were lost.

THE KING IS DEPOSED

The civil war that resulted from Richard, Duke of York's dismissal as Protector eventually led, in 1461, to Henry being deposed because of his ineffectual rule. He was replaced on the throne by Richard's son, who ruled as Edward IV until 1470, when Henry was briefly reinstated as king before being overthrown again the following year by Edward.

MURDERED IN THE TOWER

At the Battle of Tewkesbury, in May 1471, during the Wars of the Roses, Henry and his Queen, Margaret, were captured and his son Edward killed. Imprisoned in the Tower of London, he was officially found dead in bed one morning a few weeks later, but it is believed he was murdered while at prayer.

MARGARET OF ANJOU

Henry married Margaret of Anjou in 1445. Known as the 'she-wolf of France', she was quite ruthless and completely dominated the king, particularly during his bouts of mental illness. She stoutly supported the Lancashire cause in the Wars of the Roses and was imprisoned following the Battle of Tewkesbury in 1471. She was released five years later, on payment of a ransom by the French king, and died at Anjou, her homeland, in 1482.

France, and Humphrey, Duke of Gloucester, as Regent of England.

1429
Joan of Arc expels English from France.

1431
Joan of Arc burnt at stake by English.

1437
Henry VI assumes government of England

from his Regent.

1453
End of 100 Years' War - England loses all French possessions, except Calais.

1454
Henry VI suffers bout of mental illness.

1454
Richard, Duke of York, made Protector

during king's illness.

1455
Duke of York rebels against king and assumes control of government.

GOVERNMENT   HEALTH & MEDICINE   JUSTICE   RELIGION   SCIENCE

EDWARD IV

BORN 1442 • ACCEDED 1461 • DEPOSED 1470
RESTORED 1471 • DIED 1483

When Edward IV came to the throne in 1461 after defeating Henry VI at the Battle of Towton, in Yorkshire, he was just 19 years old. He was said to be a giant of a man, about 6 feet 3 inches tall when the average height was just 5 feet 4 inches. He began his reign as a genial, well-mannered diplomat, but when he died at the age of 40 he was accused of living a life of debauchery and excess.

DUKE OF CLARENCE

Edward's brother George, Duke of Clarence, had several times switched his allegiance, but Edward had always forgiven him. However, in 1478, the two brothers argued furiously and George was imprisoned in the Tower of London for treason. Although sentenced to death, the means of his execution has always been a mystery. He is popularly believed to have been drowned in a barrel of malmsey wine.

THE RIGHTFUL SUCCESSOR

Edward is generally considered to have had a stronger claim to the throne than Henry VI. His grandfather was the son of Edward III's 5th son, Edmund, and his grandmother was descended from Edward III's 3rd son, Lionel. Henry VI, on the other hand, was only descended from Edward III's 4th son, John of Gaunt.

ELIZABETH WOODVILLE

Edward married Elizabeth Woodville in 1464 and she bore him 10 children. She was the widow of a commoner, which sparked off the rift between Edward and his cousin Richard, Earl of Warwick, who feared his position at court might be undermined.

1455
Start of the Wars of the Roses.
1455
The Duke of York defeats Henry at the Battle of St. Albans.

1455
First printed Bible published in Germany.
1460
Battle of Northampton.

1460
Henry VI captured and his wife escapes to Scotland.
1461
Henry VI is deposed.

1461
Edward, Duke of York, crowned king as Edward IV.
1464
Edward marries Elizabeth Woodville.

1470
Edward driven into exile by Henry VI's supporters.
1470-71
Warwick is banished and Henry reinstated to throne.

🏛 ARCHITECTURE 📖 ARTS & LITERATURE ↪ EXPLORATION 🔥 FAMOUS BATTLES

WILLIAM CAXTON

The first printing press in England was set up by William Caxton in 1476 (left). The wooden hand-press was modelled on wine presses used in the Rhine valley and remained in use, with only minor changes, for over 350 years. Caxton, a wool merchant by trade, learned the craft of printing in Europe and he produced over 18,000 pages before he died in 1491. Books had previously to be produced by hand, which made them very expensive. Printing made books available to an ever-more literate public at reasonable cost.

COURT OF REQUESTS

Edward was a very able administrator and introduced several legal reforms, the most notable of which was the Court of Requests, where poor tenants could take complaints against greedy landlords and ask the officials to adjudicate a fair rent.

✟ ST. GEORGE'S CHAPEL

Edward built the magnificent St. George's Chapel at Windsor Castle to rival Henry VI's chapel at Eton, which could be clearly seen from the royal castle. St. George's is perhaps the finest piece of late medieval church architecture in Europe, with breath-takingly beautiful fan vaulting in the Perpendicular style.

BATTLE OF BARNET

The Battle of Barnet (below) was fought in Hertfordshire between the forces of Edward and Henry VI on Easter Day, 14th April 1471. Edward had recently returned from exile in Flanders to reassert his claim to the throne. Richard, Earl of Warwick, was killed in the battle.

INCREASED TRADE

Edward was determined to end the dreadful civil wars that had raged in England during the reign of Henry VI and restore peace and economic stability. He did a great deal to help English merchants, particularly those involved in the wool trade. England enjoyed the greatest period of prosperity this country had ever witnessed, which made him very popular with businessmen.

EXILE IN FLANDERS

In 1470 Richard, Earl of Warwick, known as 'the Kingmaker', who had earlier helped Edward onto the throne, switched his allegiance to Henry VI. Edward was forced to flee the country, to exile in Flanders, and Warwick helped Henry VI return to the throne, briefly.

1471
Henry captured at Battle of Tewkesbury.
1471
Warwick, 'the Kingmaker', defeated and killed at

Battle of Barnet.
1471
Henry VI is murdered.
1471
Edward IV, returns from exile and is proclaimed king again.

1478
Spanish Inquisition established.
1483
Edward IV dies.

🗎 GOVERNMENT   ⚕ HEALTH & MEDICINE   ⚖ JUSTICE   ✟ RELIGION   🗎 SCIENCE

EDWARD DECLARED ILLEGITIMATE

In June 1483 Parliament declared Edward V (and his brother) illegitimate and deposed him in favour of his uncle, who became Richard III. Apparently, Edward IV had already been betrothed to another at the time of his marriage to Elizabeth Woodville. Under medieval law, a betrothal carried legal status and so the marriage was declared invalid.

LUDLOW CASTLE

Edward and his brother Richard lived at Ludlow Castle, in Shropshire, from 1472 until the untimely death of their father in 1483. Ludlow Castle began as a simple Norman stronghold in about 1085. It was substantially enlarged in the 12th and 13th centuries, when it acquired an unusual circular chapel. It became royal property in 1461 when Edward Mortimer, its then owner, was crowned king as Edward IV.

EDWARD V
BORN 1470 • ACCEDED 1483 • DIED 1483(?)

When Edward IV died in 1483 the throne passed to his eldest son Edward, who was then just 13 years old. Edward's uncle Richard, Duke of Gloucester, was appointed Protector during the king's minority, according to the provisions of Edward IV's will. When both his nephews were afterwards declared illegitimate, Richard was invited by Parliament to become king as Edward IV's brother, and therefore the rightful heir. The later disappearance of the two princes is one of history's greatest mysteries.

THE PRINCES MURDERED

The last recorded sighting of the two princes was in September, in the palace gardens. They are believed to have been suffocated, by unknown assailants, in the Bloody Tower, so named after the deed. Two children's bodies were discovered at the Tower in 1674 and subsequently buried in Westminster Abbey, but forensic examination in 1933 failed to prove they were the skeletons of the princes.

1483
Edward V accedes to the throne.
1483
Richard of Gloucester (Edward's uncle) becomes

Protector of England.
1483
Edward V declared illegitimate and imprisoned in the Tower, with his brother Richard.

1483
Edward and his younger brother, Richard, believed to have been murdered in the Tower.

🏛 ARCHITECTURE   📖 ARTS & LITERATURE   ⚐ EXPLORATION   🖋 FAMOUS BATTLES

THE CASE AGAINST RICHARD III

Richard III has always been the prime suspect as being responsible for murdering the princes, though he was never accused of it in his lifetime. The accusations came later. It could be argued that, as parliament had already been convinced of their illegitimacy they were no longer a threat to his crown, so why bother murdering them? It could equally be argued, of course, that their murders removed any threats there might have been. If Richard was responsible he covered his tracks well, and today the only 'evidence' of any kind against him is in the words of Shakespeare's plays, which are largely works of fiction based loosely on fact and biased towards the Tudor propaganda machine.

THE CASE AGAINST HENRY VII

The dynastic struggle for supremacy, known as the 'Wars of the Roses', came to a head in 1485, at the Battle of Bosworth Field. The victor, Henry Tudor, who became Henry VII, defeated and killed Richard III, thus removing any further threat to the crown. Henry's claim to the throne was less valid than Richard's and so in order to make himself more acceptable as king he set about a character assassination of Richard III. It was he who first started the rumour that Richard had murdered his nephews, though he had as much, if not more, to gain by killing all Yorkist claimants to the throne, including Richard himself.

ONE OF HISTORY'S GREAT MYSTERIES

Despite the finger of suspicion having been firmly pointed at Richard III for the princes' murders, no evidence has ever come to light. No bodies have ever been proved to be the princes, so they may not have been murdered at all, but forced into hiding, particularly after the Tudor victory at Bosworth. There is an unsubstantiated tradition at Eastwell, in Kent, that a member of the royal Plantagenet family lived there in secret who may have been an illegitimate son of Richard III, or indeed, Edward V himself; we shall probably never know the truth.

IMPRISONMENT IN THE TOWER

Edward, and his younger brother Richard, travelled from Ludlow to the Tower of London, which was then the principal royal palace, in May, in preparation for the coronation. Following Edward's declared illegitimacy by parliament, the brothers were probably merely confined to their quarters, rather than being imprisoned in a dungeon.

GOVERNMENT   HEALTH & MEDICINE   JUSTICE   RELIGION   SCIENCE

RICHARD III
BORN 1452 • ACCEDED 1483 • DIED 1485

ichard, Duke of Gloucester, was appointed Protector of England during his nephew, Edward V's, minority. Within two months of Edward's coronation, he was declared illegitimate by Parliament and deposed, whether at the hands of Richard we shall never know, but as Edward IV's legitimate heir he was invited by Parliament to rule as Richard III. Richard is perhaps the most maligned figure in British history, largely as a result of the political propaganda put about by the Tudors following their usurpation of the crown in 1485. Contemporary accounts state that he was close to his brother, Edward IV, and had a kindly disposition. He was tall and considered quite handsome, and was very popular with the people.

COUNCIL OF THE NORTH

Since Norman times the north of England had received somewhat harsher treatment by the monarchy than other regions, partly fuelled by the rebellious nature of the people there who felt that their needs, so far away from the centre of government, were neglected. Richard tried to redress this imbalance by creating the Council of the North, which sought to improve the region's administration.

COLLEGE OF ARMS

The present College of Arms building in London dates from about 1670, but the college itself was founded by Richard III in 1483. The college has its origins in the group of royal retainers known as heralds, whose job it was to carry messages and arrange state occasions. The task of regulating the coats-of-arms of each noble household became part of their duties, which Richard organised into a college.

SHAKESPEARE'S IMAGE

The historical image of Richard is a far cry from the figure portrayed by Shakespeare as a deformed hunchback, a monstrous tyrant and murderer of his two nephews. Shakespeare, who was a royal favourite of his day, based his play on books written by Henry VII's supporters who, in attempting to justify their violent seizure of the crown, created the myth of an evil tyrant that still persists today.

1483
Richard III accedes to the throne after his nephew, Edward V is declared illegitimate and deposed.

1483
Duke of Buckingham leads unsuccessful rebellion against Richard.

1483
Foundation of the College of Arms.

1484
Richard's son, Edward, dies

leaving no heir.

1484
Abolition of Benevolences

ARCHITECTURE   ARTS & LITERATURE   EXPLORATION   FAMOUS BATTLES

BATTLE OF BOSWORTH FIELD

The Battle of Bosworth took place in a field outside the Leicestershire town of Market Bosworth on 22nd August 1485. Henry Tudor's army of between 7-8,000 faced a superior force of about 11-12,000. The battle could have gone either way, but when Richard III himself was killed, his supporters drifted away, leaving the Lancastrian Henry Tudor victor. It brought to a bloody close the dynastic struggle known as the 'Wars of the Roses'.

MIDDLEHAM CASTLE

Sometimes called the 'Windsor of the North', Middleham Castle, in Wensleydale, Yorkshire, was Richard's favourite residence, particularly when touring with the royal court. The present castle dates from about 1170 and contains one of the largest, and grandest, Norman keeps ever built. It passed into the Neville family about a century later. The last Neville to own it was Warwick ('the Kingmaker') and after his death at the Battle of Barnet in 1470 it passed into royal hands. Richard's only son was born and died there.

⚖ THE INTRODUCTION OF BAIL

Richard was actually a wise and very benevolent king, belying his popular image. He introduced a system of bail into court proceedings for defendants, which forms the basis of the system in use today.

📜 PARLIAMENTARY REFORMS

Richard introduced several parliamentary reforms during his short reign, the most significant perhaps being a law passed in 1484 decreeing that all future parliamentary statutes should be written in English and not French or Latin. He also abolished the practice of nobles giving compulsory gifts to the monarchy to win favour.

ANNE NEVILLE

Richard married Anne Neville in 1472. She was the daughter of Richard Neville, Earl of Warwick ('the Kingmaker'). Before Warwick's change of allegiance, their two families had been very close and they were allegedly childhood sweethearts. Middleham Castle, which Richard inherited, had been her childhood home. She died in 1485 shortly before Richard's death in battle at Bosworth.

---

prevents individuals selling favour by giving of gifts to royalty.
1484
Council of the

North created to give fairer treatment to those in the north.
1484
Bail introduced into

court system.
1484
English language used in parliamentary acts.
1485
Henry Tudor

lands in West Wales to claim the throne.
1485
Richard's queen, Anne Neville, dies.

1485
Battle of Bosworth - Richard III is defeated and killed, marking an end to the Wars of the Roses.

📋 **GOVERNMENT** 🥣 **HEALTH & MEDICINE** ⚖ **JUSTICE** ✝ **RELIGION** 📿 **SCIENCE**

WARS OF THE ROSES
(1455–1485)

A lthough usually described as a civil war, the Wars of the Roses were, more correctly, a dynastic struggle between two families with rival claims to the throne. They were really a series of intermittent battles that took place over a period of 30 years between the private armies of the claimants and did not, essentially, affect the everyday lives of the majority of the population. Both claimants were branches of the same family. Trouble first began when Henry Bolingbroke of Lancaster seized the crown from Richard II in 1399, though it was some years before it lead to outright warfare.

BLOODY BATTLES

The wars began with the Battle of St. Albans in 1455 and ended at the Battle of Bosworth in 1485. There were only 10 major skirmishes between the two sides and the total period of fighting lasted only 13 weeks. Henry VI is shown above having been captured by a subservient Earl of Warwick after the battle of Northampton, 10 July 1460.

THE WHITE ROSE OF YORK

Here, nobles are seen choosing sides in the war by picking either a red rose (Lancaster) or a white rose (York) from bushes in a garden. The Yorkists were descended from both the 3rd and 5th sons of Edward III, giving them a stronger claim to the throne.

A NEW DYNASTY-THE TUDORS

The Tudor monarchs took their name from Owain Tudor, who claimed descent from the Welsh royal family. Henry Tudor's (later Henry VII) mother was Margaret Beaufort, great-grand-daughter of John of Gaunt, of the House of Lancaster. Once established on the throne, the Tudors set about uniting a divided nation after years of civil unrest. Not always popular, they were noted for their strong government.

THE WARRIOR KING, HENRY V

Henry V, immortalised as a hero by Shakespeare, ascended the throne in 1413 at the age of 25 and immediately set about regaining his lost French lands. His most famous victory was at Agincourt in 1415, when English archers defeated the might of the French cavalry.

ARCHITECTURE   ARTS & LITERATURE   EXPLORATION   FAMOUS BATTLES

THE RED ROSE OF LANCASTER

The Lancastrian claim to the throne was through Henry, Duke of Lancaster, the son of John of Gaunt, who was the 4th son of Edward III. The Lancastrians, under Henry Tudor, eventually won the war.

THE FAMILIES UNITED

After his coronation, Henry VII (a Lancastrian) married Elizabeth of York, daughter of Edward IV, thus uniting the two families. The Tudor rose symbolised the new dynasty by incorporating both red and white roses.

HENRY VI: A WEAK MONARCH

A deeply religious man, Henry was an inept ruler who lost all of his French lands. Deposed in 1461 in favour of Edward IV, he was briefly reinstated in 1470 before being murdered the following year.

WARWICK: THE KINGMAKER

Richard Neville, Earl of Warwick, was known as 'the Kingmaker' because he was instrumental in placing Edward IV on the throne in 1461. He later engineered a plot to remove him in 1470.

MY KINGDOM FOR A HORSE

The much-maligned Richard III suffered at the hands of Tudor propagandists, including Shakespeare, but history paints him in a kinder light. He was killed at the Battle of Bosworth in 1485.

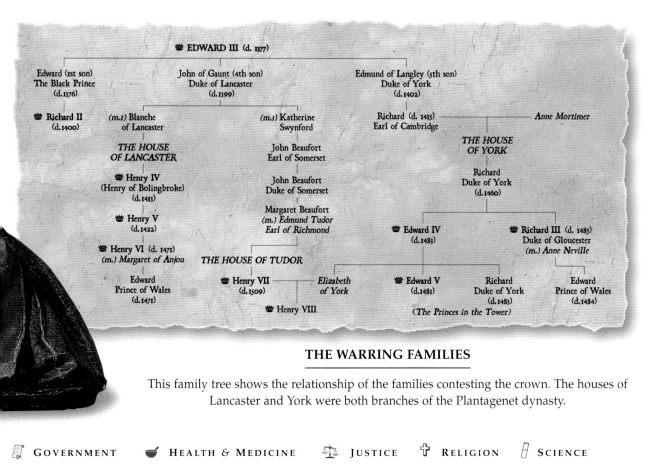

THE WARRING FAMILIES

This family tree shows the relationship of the families contesting the crown. The houses of Lancaster and York were both branches of the Plantagenet dynasty.

♔ GOVERNMENT   ⚕ HEALTH & MEDICINE   ⚖ JUSTICE   ✝ RELIGION   ⌽ SCIENCE

HENRY VII

BORN 1457 • ACCEDED 1485 • DIED 1509

espite the violent way in which he came to the throne, Henry was an advocate of peace and diplomacy; above all he was a businessman. The 'Wars of the Roses' had severely weakened the grip of the nobility and he took advantage of the situation by promoting business enterprise and encouraging merchants to expand their interests. Under his rule society changed quite radically, casting off many of the feudal ideals in favour of commercial ones. His policies certainly worked and England prospered under his rule. The Tudor period was more than just the name of a new dynasty, it marked the end of the Middle Ages. To establish his own credibility, Henry conducted a very successful 'smear campaign' to blacken the name of Richard III and may himself have been responsible for the murder of Edward V and his brother.

CLAIMANTS TO THE THRONE

For the first few years of Henry's reign he had to put down a number of Yorkist-led rebellions. Lambert Simnel (in 1487) a boy who claimed to be the Earl of Warwick and Perkin Warbeck (in 1492) who claimed to be a son of Edward IV, both led unsuccessful rebellions.

COURT OF THE STAR CHAMBER

The Court of the Star Chamber, first introduced in the 14th century as a means of controlling the power of the nobility, but which had lapsed somewhat, was revived by Henry. His purpose in doing so was two-fold. First, he felt that England must never again be subjected to the futile waste brought about by civil war, so he banned the raising of private armies. Second, he had himself gained the throne by violent means and by controlling the power of the nobility he secured his own position.

A NEW DYNASTY

Henry was the grandson of Owen Tudor, who claimed to be descended from the independent Princes of Wales. His mother was Margaret Beaufort, great-granddaughter of John of Gaunt, through whom Henry claimed the English throne.

ARTHUR, PRINCE OF WALES

Prince Arthur was the eldest son of Henry VII and had been groomed for kingship. He married Catherine of Aragon, the Spanish king's daughter, in an arranged marriage to unite the two countries. Arthur died, prematurely, in 1502, it is said, before the marriage had been consummated. When Henry died in 1509 the crown passed to his second son, Henry, who also married his dead brother's widow, Catherine, to maintain the alliance.

1485	**1485**	**1486**	*Chamber revived.*	*made in Nuremberg.*
Henry VII becomes first Tudor monarch of England after defeating Richard III at Bosworth.	*Henry forms Yeomen of the Guard as a personal bodyguard service to protect him.*	*Henry marries Elizabeth of York, uniting the houses of Lancaster and York.*	**1487** *Revolt led by Lambert Simnel put down.*	**1491** *Henry VII invades France.*
		1487 *Court of the Star*	**c.1490** *First modern globe*	**1491** *Treaty of Etaples, Henry agrees to withdraw from*

🏛 ARCHITECTURE 📖 ARTS & LITERATURE ⛵ EXPLORATION 🔥 FAMOUS BATTLES

CHRISTOPHER COLUMBUS

Christopher Columbus approached Henry for patronage when he embarked upon his voyages of discovery in the 'New World'. Henry was keen to develop business interests outside of war-torn Europe and considered sponsoring Columbus who, in 1492, re-discovered America.

THE NEW WORLD

Unshackled by the old ideals, the Tudor age really was an age of adventure. Henry was keen to patronise anyone who might further England's prosperity by opening up new trade routes. From 1496 on, Henry sponsored John Cabot, a Venetian who had settled in England, and his three sons to seek out new lands, in return for which he demanded one-fifth of any profits.

PEACE AT LAST

Following Henry's victory at Bosworth, there were several attempts on his life. He responded by forming the Yeomen of the Guard, early in 1485, as personal bodyguards in the royal palace. The red livery of their uniforms is still a familiar sight at the Tower of London today. Henry was a great patron of the arts and encouraged the English Renaissance - the 'revival of learning' - among artists and scholars in the relative peace of his reign.

PEMBROKE CASTLE

Henry was born at Pembroke Castle in South Wales, a magnificent Norman stronghold and seat of the Marshals, Earls of Pembroke. He spent 15 years at Pembroke before being forced to flee to Brittany. He returned to Milford Haven in 1485 to claim the English throne.

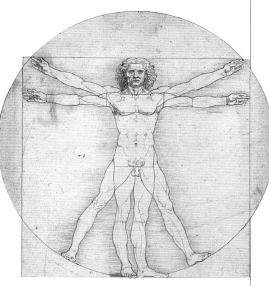

ELIZABETH OF YORK

Within six months of acceding to the throne, Henry (a Lancastrian) married Elizabeth of York, uniting the two warring families and so bringing to an end 30 years of civil war. Despite their obvious political differences it was, by all accounts, a happy marriage and she bore him eight children.

LEONARDO DA VINCI

Leonardo da Vinci (1452-1519) was at the forefront of the Renaissance movement in art and learning. Born in Florence, da Vinci was an artist, an architect and a scientist, whose revolutionary ideas greatly influenced Henry. His most famous work of art is probably the 'Mona Lisa' and the 'Vitruvian Man' is shown above.

France in payment of large sum of cash.	**1492** *Christopher Columbus rediscovers America.*	*sponsored by Henry.* **1499** *Perkin Warbeck is executed.*	*Arthur, dies.* **1502** *First spring-driven watch invented.*	*Margaret, marries James IV of Scotland, uniting the Tudor and Stuart dynasties.*
1492 *Perkin Warbeck claims throne and leads a revolt against Henry.*	**1497** *The Cabot brothers sail to North America,*	**1502** *Henry's eldest son, and heir, Prince*	**1502** *Henry's eldest daughter,*	**1509** *Henry VII dies.*

📕 GOVERNMENT　　🥣 HEALTH & MEDICINE　　⚖ JUSTICE　　✝ RELIGION　　▯ SCIENCE

HENRY VIII
BORN 1491 • ACCEDED 1509 • DIED 1547

*H*enry VIII came to the throne at the age of 17. He was a flamboyant character who had not been groomed for kingship and only came to the throne because of the premature death of his elder brother Arthur, in 1502. Well liked at first, he became something of a tyrant in later years, particularly if he did not get his own way. Despite being one of our more well-known monarchs, he was not a great king and is best remembered for breaking with the Church of Rome and for marrying six times.

ILL-HEALTH AND OLD AGE

Henry was plagued by ill-health in later years. He suffered from obesity, severe headaches, smallpox, syphilis, thrombosis and ulcerated legs. He was also grossly overweight and had to be carried up and down stairs using a hoist.

YOUNG HENRY

As a young man Henry was a robust, athletic man standing 6ft. (1.83 metres) tall. He preferred to spend his time at sports or leisure activities, leaving governance of the country to a group of trusted advisers.

THOMAS WOLSEY

Cardinal Thomas Wolsey (1475-1530) was of humble birth but quickly rose to become one of Henry's most trusted advisers. He was made chancellor in 1514 and virtually governed the country in the early years of Henry's reign, but fell from favour when he failed to secure Henry's divorce from Catherine of Aragon. He was arrested, but died en route to the Tower of London.

MUSICAL PROWESS

Henry VIII was a keen patron of the arts and was himself an accomplished singer and musician. He could play several instruments to quite a high standard, including the harp, organ, virginals (a harpsichord-like instrument) and the lute, shown here. He also composed several tunes including, it is believed, 'Greensleeves'.

1509
Henry VIII succeeds to the throne.

1509
Henry marries Catherine of Aragon, his dead brother's widow.

1513
English defeat Scots at Battle of Flodden Field, killing James IV.

1515
Thomas Wolsey elected Chancellor.

c.1515
Coffee first introduced into Europe.

1516
Queen Catherine gives birth to a girl (later Mary I).

1517
Martin Luther publishes treatise on anti-Catholicism.

1519/22
The Portuguese Ferdinand Magellan first person to circumnavigate the world.

1520
'Field of the Cloth of Gold',

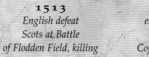

🏛 ARCHITECTURE   📖 ARTS & LITERATURE   ⚑ EXPLORATION   💣 FAMOUS BATTLES

PERSECUTIONS

As Henry's reign wore on he became ever more obsessive and tyrannical. He removed from office anyone who stood in his way and ordered the executions of several thousand people - indeed, one estimate puts the figure as high as 50,000!

THOMAS MORE

Sir Thomas More was Henry's Lord Chancellor and chief minister at the time of his application to annul his marriage to Catherine. He was also a devout Catholic and refused to acknowledge Henry as head of the new English Church following the break with Rome, for which he was executed in 1535, causing a public outcry.

BREAK WITH THE CHURCH OF ROME

There was a growing band of people, called Protestants, who disagreed with many of the Catholic doctrines and who sought church reforms. When the pope refused to annul Henry's marriage to Catherine of Aragon the Protestants seized upon the opportunity to establish a new church and lent their support to the king. Although England eventually broke away from the Church of Rome, Henry himself remained a Catholic. The Church of England did not become fully Protestant until Elizabeth I's reign.

⚫ BATTLE OF FLODDEN FIELD

In 1513 James IV of Scotland invaded northern England in support of the French, with whom Henry was at war. James and many of the Scottish nobility were routed and killed at the Battle of Flodden Field.

✝ MARTIN LUTHER (1483-1546)

Martin Luther was a church reformer from Germany who objected to what he considered corruption within the Catholic Church, for which he was excommunicated. Henry spoke out against Luther's 'Protestant' writings in a book, published in 1521. Ironically, the pope honoured Henry with the title 'Defender of the Faith'. Twelve years later Henry broke with the Church of Rome himself.

✝ DISSOLUTION OF THE MONASTERIES

By Henry's time many of the monastic ideals had become somewhat lax so, as head of the new Church of England, he seized upon the opportunity to close them down and claim their wealth. Many of the charges levelled against the monks were false, but between 1536-40 Thomas Cromwell, acting as Henry's agent, closed down, or 'dissolved', all of the monasteries, claiming all their lands and possessions for the crown.

📜 ACT OF SUPREMACY

In 1533 parliament passed the Act of Appeals, which asserted England's independence from the Church of Rome. It was ratified the following year with the Act of Supremacy, which made Henry 'Supreme Head of the Church of England'.

peace talks between Henry and France.

1525
William Tyndale publishes translation of the New Testament.

1529
Cardinal Wolsey accused of high treason, dies whilst awaiting trial.

c.1530
First coalmines in England

open in Newcastle.

1533
Henry's marriage to Catherine of Aragon is annulled by Archbishop Thomas Cranmer.

1533
Henry marries Anne Boleyn.

1533
Anne gives birth to a girl (later Elizabeth I).

1533
Henry is excommunicated.

1534
Act of Supremacy establishes Henry as head of new Church of England.

CATHERINE OF ARAGON

BORN 1485 • MARRIED 1509 • DIVORCED 1533 • DIED 1536

Catherine of Aragon was the daughter of King Ferdinand of Spain. She was beautiful, intelligent and fun-loving and was betrothed to Henry VII's eldest son Arthur to form an Anglo-Spanish alliance. They married in 1501 but within six months she was widowed. In 1509 she married Henry VIII, initially to keep the alliance but they are said to have genuinely loved one another and remained happily married for 20 years. She gave birth to several children but only one, Princess Mary, survived. It was only after her inability to conceive a son and heir for Henry that he commenced divorce proceedings. He originally tried to have the marriage annulled on the grounds that as his sister-in-law it was an unlawful union. The pope denied Henry so he broke with the Church of Rome and divorced her in 1533. She was banished from court and died three years later.

ANNE BOLEYN

BORN 1502 • MARRIED 1533 • DIVORCED 1536 • EXECUTED 1536

When it became clear that Catherine was not going to give him the son he so desperately wanted, Henry began to take several mistresses including the queen's young lady-in-waiting, Anne Boleyn. Henry courted her at her family home, Hever Castle, in Kent, and they married in secret in January 1533, four months before his divorce from Catherine was finalised. She gave birth to Princess Elizabeth in September of the same year. When Anne too failed to deliver him a son he commenced divorce proceedings against her also. She was accused of adultery with, amongst others, her own brother. The marriage was annulled on 17th May 1536 and two days later Henry had her executed.

JANE SEYMOUR

BORN 1509 • MARRIED 1536 • DIED 1537

When Anne Boleyn also failed to give Henry a son he began to cast his eye towards her lady-in-waiting, Jane Seymour. At first Jane declined his advances and insisted on being chaperoned in his presence. They were married just two weeks after Anne Boleyn's execution. In October the following year, 1537, Jane gave birth to a son, Edward, by Caesarean section. Complications set in and Jane died of blood poisoning two weeks later. Henry was heartbroken by her death and would probably have remained faithful to her, had she lived.

MARRIAGE STAKES

This timeline (below) shows that although Henry married six times, over two thirds of his reign was spent with his first wife Catherine of Aragon. He married all of his other five wives in the last 11 years of his reign.

YEARS OF MARRIAGE

Anne of Cleves 6months

Catherine of Aragon 24yrs

Anne Boleyn 3yrs

Jane Seymour 1yr

Catherine Howard 2yrs

Catherine Parr 5yrs

1509

1547

🏛 ARCHITECTURE   📖 ARTS & LITERATURE   ⚑ EXPLORATION   ⬤ FAMOUS BATTLES

THE SIX WIVES OF HENRY VIII

Henry VIII is perhaps best remembered in history for being our most married monarch. He married six times, the first three of which were said to be genuine love matches. The last three were purely political or for reasons of expediency. Henry became obsessed with producing a male heir ('the king's great matter'). He had been happily married to Catherine of Aragon for the first 20 years of his reign and married all of the other five within the last 11 years.

CATHERINE HOWARD

BORN 1521 • MARRIED 1540
EXECUTED 1542

Henry seems to have developed a liking for his current queen's lady-in-waiting. He took an instant liking to Anne of Cleves' lady servant, Catherine Howard, the Duke of Norfolk's niece. She was high-spirited and flirtatious, which at first aroused Henry's interest, but later was the cause of his jealousy. She married Henry just 16 days after the king's divorce from Anne, but less than two years later she was executed, at the young age of 21, accused of adultery, unseemly behaviour and treason.

ANNE OF CLEVES

BORN 1515 • MARRIED 1540
DIVORCED 1540 • DIED 1557

Following Jane Seymour's death Henry might not have married again, especially as he now had the son he had so long craved, but he was placed under mounting political pressure by Thomas Cromwell and other ministers to marry again. Reluctantly he agreed to a marriage of convenience to the German princess, Anne of Cleves, forming an alliance between Germany and England to ward off a threatened Franco-Spanish invasion to re-establish papal power. Henry disliked her intensely, calling her the 'Flanders Mare', and refused to consummate the marriage. They were divorced just six months later.

CATHERINE PARR

BORN 1512 • MARRIED 1543 • DIED 1548

Catherine Parr was a quiet, well-educated lady of comparatively mature years (when she married Henry), in stark contrast to her predecessors. Henry was by that time suffering from several serious ailments and Catherine acted more as a nurse than a wife. Henry was fond of her and appreciated the sense of calm she brought to the royal household. Already twice widowed before marrying Henry, she married again soon after his death, but died the following year during childbirth.

1536 Anne Boleyn accused of adultery and executed.	Jane Seymour. **1537** Queen Jane gives birth to a boy (later Edward VI).	following complications after childbirth. **1540** Henry marries Anne of Cleves, divorces her later the same year.	**1540** Henry marries Catherine Howard.	**1543** Henry marries his sixth wife, Catherine Parr.
1536 Henry marries	**1537** Jane Seymour dies		**1542** Catherine is accused of treason and executed.	**1547** Henry VIII dies.

GOVERNMENT   HEALTH & MEDICINE   JUSTICE   RELIGION   SCIENCE

EDWARD VI

BORN 1537 • ACCEDED 1547 • DIED 1553
& LADY JANE GREY
BORN 1537 • ACCEDED 1553 • DEPOSED 1553 (*9 days later*) • EXECUTED 1553

dward was the only legitimate son of Henry VIII to survive. Until about the age of five or six he was brought up in the royal nursery, with his half-sister, Elizabeth, but from then on he was groomed for his future role as king by John Cheke. Because his father had remained a Catholic, even after the break with Rome, Edward was the first Protestant monarch of England and under his rule the Reformation of the English Church was consolidated.

BOY KING

Edward succeeded to the throne at the age of nine. During his minority the country was governed by a Protector. Edward was a sickly child with many of his father's arrogant mannerisms. In January 1553 he contracted tuberculosis and died six months later, aged 15.

GREENWICH PALACE

The Tudor palace of Placentia stood on the banks of the Thames at Greenwich, then a small village in the countryside surrounding London. It was a great favourite of the Tudor monarchs and is where Edward died in 1553. It was rebuilt by Charles II and later extended and converted for use as a naval hospital, college and maritime museum.

THE PROTECTORS

THE DUKE OF SOMERSET
The first Protector appointed to govern during Edward's minority was his uncle, Edward Seymour, Earl of Hertford, later created Duke of Somerset. Unpopular with many of the nobles, he was deposed in 1550 and executed two years later.

THE DUKE OF NORTHUMBERLAND
Following Seymour's deposition, John Dudley, Earl of Warwick, was appointed as Edward's Protector. He created himself Duke of Northumberland and manipulated the young king to suit his own ends. He contrived to marry his son, Lord Guildford Dudley, to Lady Jane Grey and then persuaded the dying Edward (shown here on the day of his coronation) to proclaim Jane queen on his death. When Mary I overthrew Jane and proclaimed herself queen, Northumberland was executed.

1546	1547	an ill-fated plan to	Edward, Seymour,	1549
Henry VIII's last will confirms the line of succession on his death as Edward, followed by Mary, then Elizabeth.	*Edward VI accedes to the throne.* **1547** *English defeat Scots at Battle of Pinkie, as part of*	*place Mary Queen of Scotts on the English throne.* **1547** *Edward's uncle,*	*(Duke of Somerset) becomes Protector of England.* **1548** *Catherine Parr dies.*	*First Act of Uniformity bans Roman Catholic mass.* **1549** *First Book of Common Prayer published.*

🏛 ARCHITECTURE   📖 ARTS & LITERATURE   ⚑ EXPLORATION   💣 FAMOUS BATTLES

A QUEEN FOR NINE DAYS

Lady Jane Grey is one of the tragic figures of English history, an innocent pawn in the often violent and devious power struggles surrounding the line of succession to the throne. She was the Protestant daughter of Frances, Duchess of Suffolk, and Henry VIII's great-niece. An intelligent, quiet and beautiful girl, she became a good friend of Edward, her cousin. When Edward lay on his deathbed he was persuaded by his Protector John Dudley, Duke of Northumberland, to name Jane as his successor to ensure that the throne remained in Protestant hands. Jane reluctantly agreed, but ruled for just nine days, in July 1553, before being taken prisoner by Mary, Edward's half-sister and rightful heir. She was executed the following year when just 17 years old.

LINE OF SUCCESSION

On 30th December 1546 Henry VIII made his last will (right) in which he settled the line of succession. Sensing perhaps that his own death was imminent, he may also have had reservations about the health of his son and made provision for, first Mary and then Elizabeth, to succeed Edward should he die.

🗒 ACT OF UNIFORMITY

The Reformation of the church that had been instigated by Henry VIII was consolidated by parliament during Edward's reign, overseen by the king's Protector, Edward Seymour, Duke of Somerset. The first Act of Uniformity was passed in 1549 which banned the Catholic mass and demanded all paintings and idolatry be removed from churches.

✟ BOOK OF COMMON PRAYER

The First Book of Common Prayer was written by Thomas Cranmer (above), Archbishop of Canterbury, and published in 1549. For the first time the mass was read in English instead of Latin, which greatly offended many Catholics who disagreed with the Reformation. Many riots broke out around the country, which were put down by force.

💣 BATTLE OF PINKIE

When Henry VIII died the Scots took the opportunity to try to unite the two countries by forcing Edward to marry his Catholic cousin Mary, Queen of Scots. The English army thwarted the attempt and defeated the Scots at the Battle of Pinkie in 1547.

1549 Church services changed from Latin to English. **1550** Duke of Somerset	deposed and replaced by John Dudley, Earl of Warwick. **1551** Leonard Digges invents the theodolite.	**1552** Duke of Somerset is executed. **1553** Edward contracts tuberculosis.	**1553** Edward VI dies. **1553** Lady Jane Grey is proclaimed queen; she rules for nine days.	**1553** Lady Jane Grey is arrested by Mary I when she accedes to the throne.

✝ PROTESTANT BISHOPS EXECUTED

As part of her policy to return England to Catholicism, Mary rescinded all anti-Catholic laws introduced by Edward VI and replaced all of the Protestant bishops. Three of the leading Protestant clergymen, Nicholas Ridley (Bishop of London), Hugh Latimer and Thomas Cranmer (Archbishop of Canterbury) were burnt at the stake for heresy.

SMITHFIELD MARTYRS

Altogether, Mary is believed to have had nearly 300 Protestants executed. The largest mass execution, and the one which so repulsed the population, was at Smithfield in London, in 1555, when 43 martyrs were burnt at the stake. Excavations in 1849, near St. Bartholomew's Hospital, revealed charred oak posts and human remains. A memorial was set up at the hospital.

RESTORATION OF CATHOLICISM

Although she had been forced to acknowledge her parents' divorce and sign the oath of succession, Mary wrote secretly to the pope stating that she was forced to do so and would revert the country to Catholicism should she ever accede to the throne. She revived the laws of heresy but many refused to acknowledge papal authority. She excused her cruel behaviour by saying that it was necessary to save their souls from the evil of Protestantism.

MARRIAGE TO PHILIP OF SPAIN

Mary married Philip of Spain in July 1554, partly to form an alliance with Spain and partly to strengthen the return to Catholicism, but it was an unhappy marriage and produced no children. Philip spent hardly any time with her in England and when he succeeded to the Spanish throne in 1556 he left England and never returned.

1553 Lady Jane Grey is proclaimed Protestant successor by the Protector, the Duke of Northumberland,	*but she is arrested and imprisoned by Mary 9 days later.* **1553** *Mary I accedes to the throne on*	*the death of her younger brother, Edward VI.* **1554** *Mary marries the Catholic, Philip of Spain.*	**1554** *Sir Thomas Wyatt leads rebellion against Mary's marriage to Philip of Spain.*	**1554** *Wyatt and Lady Jane Grey executed.* **1554** *Mary reverts England to Catholicism.*

ARCHITECTURE   **ARTS & LITERATURE**   **EXPLORATION**   **FAMOUS BATTLES**

MARY I

BORN 1516 • ACCEDED 1553 • DIED 1558

Mary I was probably one of our most unpopular monarchs. She was the daughter of Henry VIII by his first wife, Catherine of Aragon, a Spaniard, and was brought up a devout Catholic. She became embittered when her parents were divorced and her accession to the throne was denied. When Edward VI died in 1553 she was again passed over in favour of Lady Jane Grey. Not to be denied this time, however, she marched on London and deposed Jane.

LOSS OF CALAIS

In 1557 Mary declared war on France, but it was short-lived. The following year the French successfully took Calais, the last remaining English possession in France.

WYATT'S REBELLION

Many people objected to Mary's marriage and at having a Catholic foreigner sharing the English throne. Sir Thomas Wyatt, Sheriff of Kent, led a rebellion in protest at the marriage in 1554. He had initial success, defeating a royal army at Strood and capturing Cooling Castle, in Kent, but the rebellion was badly organised and later collapsed. Wyatt was executed at the Tower of London for treason.

'BLOODY MARY'

A bitter, morose woman, Mary frequently incurred the wrath of Henry VIII and refused to acknowledge her half-sister, Princess Elizabeth. Under her rule Protestants were cruelly persecuted and many were burned at the stake for heresy, earning her the title, 'Bloody Mary'.

CARDINAL REGINALD POLE

Cardinal Reginald Pole, a loyal and faithful Catholic, was appointed Archbishop of Canterbury in 1556 after the Protestant bishops had been deposed. His intention was to reverse all of the recent church reforms and restore the pope as supreme head of the church in England. However, he died shortly after Mary in 1558 before many of his policies could be implemented.

1554-58
Persecution of Protestants with the revival of laws heresy.

1555
Three Protestant

bishops burned at the stake for heresy.

1556
Cranmer, former Archbishop of

Canterbury, executed.

1556
Cardinal Reginald Pole is appointed Archbishop of Canterbury.

1556
Philip becomes king of Spain; leaves England.

1557
England declares war with France.

1558
England loses Calais, last possession in France.

1558
Mary I dies, childless.

GOVERNMENT   HEALTH & MEDICINE   JUSTICE   RELIGION   SCIENCE

ELIZABETH I

BORN 1533 • ACCEDED 1558 • DIED 1603

THE VIRGIN QUEEN

Elizabeth never married, despite being courted by several very eligible suitors, including Robert Dudley, Earl of Leicester, and Robert Devereux, 2nd Earl of Essex. She chose instead to remain a virgin and devote her life to governing the country. She once said that she was married to the 'Kingdom of England'.

THE BARD OF AVON

William Shakespeare (1564-1616) was at the forefront of the English Renaissance in art and literature. Best known as a playwright, he began his career first as a stage-hand and then as an actor in the theatre. He sometimes gave personal readings of his plays to Elizabeth in her private chambers.

EARL OF ESSEX

Robert Devereux, Second Earl of Essex, was another of Elizabeth's favourites. Although 34 years her junior the queen is said to have genuinely loved him. He used his position at court to further his political career. He betrayed her trust, however, and was executed for treason in 1601.

The daughter of Henry VIII and Anne Boleyn, Elizabeth could never have expected to become queen. Third in line to the throne, she spent much of her early life at Hatfield House, in Hertfordshire. In 1554 she was briefly imprisoned in the Tower of London because of her suspected involvement in Thomas Wyatt's rebellion.

Although she was a Protestant, she diluted many of the extremes of the church reforms to make them more acceptable. She came to the throne at age 25 and was successful in uniting a bitterly divided country. Her reign is marked by its stability. It was an age of adventure and discovery and England prospered as never before, laying the foundations of the British Empire.

EARL OF LEICESTER

Robert Dudley, Earl of Leicester, was one of Elizabeth's favourites at court. He entertained her at Kenilworth Castle in 1575 for 19 days and once asked for her hand in marriage, but she refused him.

1558
Elizabeth I accedes to the throne.
1559
Act of Supremacy restores Protestantism and

establishes Elizabeth as head of Church of England.
1562
Francis Drake makes first slave-trading voyage to America.

1564
Birth of William Shakespeare.
1568
Mary Queen of Scots flees to England in exile;

imprisoned by Elizabeth.
1577/80
Francis Drake completes first circumnavigation of the world by an Englishman.

1580
Elizabeth excommunicated by the pope.
1583
John Somerville attempts to assassinate Elizabeth.

🏛 ARCHITECTURE   📖 ARTS & LITERATURE   ⚑ EXPLORATION   💣 FAMOUS BATTLES

POOR LAW

In 1601 a Poor Law was passed in Parliament which imposed a poor relief rate on the wealthy to help keep those who could not work because they were blind, sick or crippled. Those who were capable of work, but chose to live as vagabonds, were punished. Poor people receiving relief had to stay within their own parish.

MARY QUEEN OF SCOTS

The Tudors were related to the Stuarts, royal family of Scotland. Elizabeth's cousin Mary, a Catholic and queen of Scotland, was involved in a plot to place her on the English throne. Aware that Mary had been implicated against her will, Elizabeth was reluctant to sign her death warrant, which she did, eventually, after 19 years of imprisonment, in 1587. Elizabeth never married and when she died in 1603 the throne passed to Mary's son, James VI of Scotland (James I of England) as her closest relative.

WAR WITH SPAIN

Ever since Henry VIII's break with the Church of Rome, England was placed under threat of invasion from the Catholic countries of Europe to re-establish papal authority. Elizabeth had refused Philip II's (her brother-in-law) hand in marriage and, as the most powerful country in Europe at that time, Spain needed little encouragement to lead the proposed invasion. Elizabeth gave her permission for her sea captains to perform acts of piracy against Spanish ships, further antagonising Philip. They preyed successfully on the slow and cumbersome galleons, an example of which is shown here.

DRAKE'S CIRCUMNAVIGATION

Francis Drake circumnavigated the world between 1577-80, the first Englishman to do so. On his return he was greeted with a hero's welcome and was knighted by Elizabeth aboard his ship, the 'Golden Hind' (shown left).

ACT OF SUPREMACY

A further Act of Supremacy, passed in 1559, re-established the monarchy as Supreme Head of the Church in England, following Mary's attempts to re-establish papal authority in England.

THE SPANISH ARMADA

Spain sent a massive armada in 1588 as the first stage in a proposed invasion of England. The daring seamanship of Drake, Frobisher, Hawkins and others outmanoeuvred the Spanish fleet, which was routed in a week-long running battle in the Channel. Of 138 ships that set out from Spain, only 67 returned, escaping only by sailing north, around the coasts of Scotland and Ireland.

WALTER RALEIGH

Sir Walter Raleigh, like Drake, Frobisher and other seafaring adventurers, opened up new trade routes in the unexplored regions of the world, bringing home untold riches and exotic goods, such as potatoes, chillies (below) and tobacco. He fell from favour under James I, however, and was executed for treason in 1618.

1587	1592	*first trip to South America.*	*leaves for England, but is*	1601
Mary Queen of Scots is executed.	*John David discovers the Falkland Islands, off the Argentinean coast.*	1596 *Sir Francis Drake dies of dysentery in the Caribbean.*	*scattered by bad weather.* 1599 *The Edict of Nantes in France grants freedom to Protestants.*	*Robert Devereux, Earl of Essex, executed.* 1603
1588 *Spanish Armada defeated*	1595 *Sir Walter Raleigh makes his*	1597 *Second Spanish Armada*		*Elizabeth I dies; last Tudor monarch.*

GOVERNMENT   HEALTH & MEDICINE   JUSTICE   RELIGION   SCIENCE

JAMES I

BORN 1566 • ACCEDED 1603 • DIED 1625

'THE WISEST FOOL IN CHRISTENDOM'

Although James was a well-educated and learned man, it is difficult to take him seriously as a great monarch. He was something of a scholar and wrote various treatises including one on witchcraft and another on the evils of smoking tobacco, but he seemed unable to focus either his wit or his intelligence. His governance was weak and he relied heavily on his favourites at court, earning him the nickname 'the wisest fool in Christendom', given to him by the Spanish ambassador Count Gondomar.

THE KING'S FAVOURITES

One of the principal reasons for James's unpopularity, both at court and with his people, was his choice of favourite advisers, Robert Kerr, created Earl of Somerset, and George Villiers, who later became Duke of Buckingham. Kerr encouraged James to make peace with the hated Spanish, while Buckingham became so powerful that as the king sank into senility in later life he virtually ruled the country unaided.

ames's parents were Mary Queen of Scots and Henry Stewart, Lord Darnley. He succeeded to the Scottish throne as James VI when just a few months old. He was Henry VII's great-great-grandson and Elizabeth I's closest relation when she died in 1603. When he was crowned King James I of England he thus united the crowns of Scotland and England. He was, by all accounts, a small, awkward and very ungainly man who had a speech impediment, caused by having a tongue too large for his mouth. His manners and personal hygiene were atrocious. It is claimed he never washed and his skin reputedly felt like black satin.

DIVINE RIGHT OF KINGS

James had ruled in Scotland as James VI for 36 years under the doctrine of the 'Divine Right of Kings', which held that kings were appointed by God and were beyond judgement from their fellow men. For the English this was an unacceptable form of government. Parliament had long campaigned to reduce the power of the monarchy and when James ruled for long periods without Parliament he became increasingly unpopular. In 1605 an attempt was made to assassinate him.

RALEIGH EXECUTED

Sir Walter Raleigh, who had been one of Elizabeth I's favourites, fell from grace under James I. He was convicted on a trumped-up charge of treason in 1603, but his execution was commuted to imprisonment because of his popularity. Released after 15 years to take part in the ill-fated voyage to discover El Dorado, he was executed in 1618 for attacking the Spanish.

1603
James VI of Scotland
is crowned James I
of England.
1603
Sir Walter Raleigh arrested

for treason and imprisoned
for 15 years.
1604
Somerset House Peace
Conference between
England and Spain.

1604
James commissions
new English translation
of Bible.
1604
Hampton Court Conference

between Anglicans
and Puritans.
1605
Gunpowder Plot, attempt
by Catholic rebels to blow
up Parliament.

1607
Irish rebellion against
English rule put down.
1607
Northern Ireland
settled by Protestants

🏛 ARCHITECTURE   📖 ARTS & LITERATURE   ⚑ EXPLORATION   🔥 FAMOUS BATTLES

PEACE CONFERENCE

The Scots had frequently formed an alliance with Spain against England, their common enemy, and within a year of acceding to the English throne James initiated peace talks with Spain. The talks culminated in a peace conference in 1604, held at Somerset House, in London, between English and Spanish diplomats.

PROTESTANTS COLONISE ULSTER

Following the collapse of the Irish rebellion, led by the Earls of Tyrone and Tyrconnel, Ulster was colonised by English and Scottish Protestants. Although England and Ireland had long been at war, albeit intermittently, it was this act, perhaps more than any other, that led to the religious and political divisions within Ireland, laying the foundations for the modern 'troubles'.

ANNE OF DENMARK

James married Anne of Denmark in Oslo in 1589 and together they had nine children. The Queen's House, at Greenwich, was begun by him as an out-of-town residence for Anne, but was abandoned on her death. Today, it forms part of the National Maritime Museum complex and contains a fine collection of contemporary paintings and furnishings.

⚑ THE PILGRIM FATHERS

James told the Puritans, an extra zealous group of Protestants, that if they did not conform to the Church of England they would be 'harried from the land'. A small group of them, unwilling to conform, fled to Holland to escape persecution in 1608 and 12 years later set sail for the new colony of Virginia, in North America. After several false starts, the group of Puritans, known as the Pilgrim Fathers, set sail for America from Plymouth on 16th September 1620 aboard the 'Mayflower'. Life in the new colony was harsh, but they instigated a system of self-government which formed the basis for the American system of government.

📖 SHAKESPEARE'S SONNETS

William Shakespeare (1564–1616), although better known as a playwright, wrote his plays in iambic pentameter (a form of verse) and also wrote a series of sonnets, or love poems, published in 1609. Sonnets were short, 14-line poems introduced into England from Italy by Sir Thomas Wyatt.

✝ AUTHORISED VERSION OF THE BIBLE

In 1604 James commissioned 54 scholars to write a new translation of the Bible. It was written in everyday English, using a vocabulary of just 5,000 words, and published in 1611. For nearly four centuries it has remained the most widely read book in the English language. Ironically, although intended to unite the divided religious beliefs of the nation, by promoting individual conscience and judgement, it led to the development of Puritanism and was instrumental in causing the Civil War of 1642–9.

📜 GOVERNMENT ⚕ HEALTH & MEDICINE ⚖ JUSTICE ✝ RELIGION 🧪 SCIENCE

Bates · Robert Winter · Christopher Wright · John Wright · Thomas Percy · Guido (Guy) Fawkes · Sir Robert Catesby · Thomas Winter

THE CONSPIRATORS

Altogether there were 12 conspirators in the plot. They were led by Sir Robert Catesby who, along with others, had already taken part in one ill-fated rebellion when they sided with the Earl of Essex against Elizabeth I. Among the conspirators was a man called John Johnson, who was born a Protestant but later converted to Catholicism. He was an explosives expert who had been fighting in Flanders for the Spanish army and who was given the responsibility of setting the charge beneath Parliament. He afterwards confessed, under torture, to being one Guido (Guy) Fawkes.

THE FAILED ATTEMPT

One of the conspirators, Thomas Percy, had connections at court, which he used to rent a house near the House of Lords where he could store his fuel stocks. From there they dug a tunnel beneath the Parliament building and filled it with barrels of gunpowder. Suspicions had already been aroused prior to the eventual discovery and a 24-hour watch was mounted on the cellar by the conspirators.

BETRAYAL AND CAPTURE

The plotters made a fatal mistake by showing compassion towards fellow Catholics who they knew would be sitting in Parliament on the intended day of the explosion. A secret message was sent to one of the conspirators' brother-in-law, Lord Monteagle, warning him to avoid attending the state opening, but he informed the Privy Council. Lord Suffolk conducted a search of the cellars and uncovered the plot at about midnight on 4th November.

🏠 ARCHITECTURE   📖 ARTS & LITERATURE   🏳 EXPLORATION   ⬤ FAMOUS BATTLES

THE GUNPOWDER PLOT

1605

Although perhaps the most remembered and commemorated event in British history, the Gunpowder Plot is shrouded in mystery. As a Protestant, James I was under considerable pressure to strengthen the throne by introducing strict, anti-Catholic laws. The traditional view is that a group of Catholic nobles attempted to assassinate the king and destroy his Protestant Parliament, but many now believe the whole plot was a Protestant contrivance to justify their harsh treatment of the Catholics.

BACKGROUND TO THE PLOT

James I was an unpopular king, particularly with the Catholics, who petitioned him for fairer treatment but were ignored. There had already been several failed attempts to depose him in 1603, after which a plot was devised to blow up the king during the state opening of Parliament in February 1605. Unfortunately, the opening was put back until November, which increased the risk of detection.

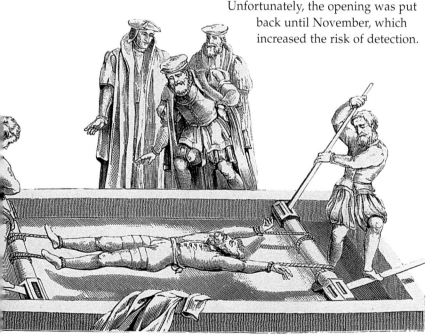

TORTURE

On hearing news that the plot had been discovered, several of the conspirators fled London, only to be later captured by the authorities. Catesby and three others were killed, while the remaining eight were arrested. They were first tortured, then tried and executed by being hanged, drawn and quartered.

BONFIRE NIGHT

The Gunpowder Plot is still commemorated with bonfire celebrations and firework displays every 5th November, the date when Parliament would have been destroyed.

PAGAN OVERTONES

It has often been claimed that the Gunpowder Plot was contrived by the authorities to justify the harsh treatment of Catholics by the Protestant government, but there may also be pagan overtones. Many aspects of the pagan, pre-Christian religion were still widely practised, but 'Christianised' by the church to make them acceptable. All-Hallows Eve was an ancient 'fire festival' when livestock was slaughtered for the onset of winter, at which a sacrifice was originally made. The festival may have been 'Christianised' by shifting the emphasis to celebrating the uncovering of the Gunpowder Plot. It is interesting to note that men called 'guisers' lit the fires at pagan festivals and the conspirator John Johnson only confessed to being 'Guido Fawkes' on being tortured, so the whole thing may have been a contrivance, with the burning of the guy replacing the ritual sacrifice.

GOVERNMENT   HEALTH & MEDICINE   JUSTICE   RELIGION   SCIENCE

💣 CIVIL WAR

The arguments that had raged between the monarchy and Parliament for several centuries finally came to a head during the reign of Charles I, when civil war broke out between 1642-49.

⚖️ PETITION OF RIGHT

In 1628 Charles was forced to acknowledge the 'Petition of Right', giving certain rights and liberties to Parliament and challenging royal power. Its four main demands were: taxation should be levied only with parliamentary consent; no-one should be jailed without trial; martial law should be abolished and no troops should be billeted in private households.

📖 VAN DYCK

The painter Anthony Van Dyck was born in the Spanish Netherlands, in what is now Belgium, in 1599. His revolutionary style of portraiture caught the eye of Charles I, who invited him to live in England as the court painter, where he remained until his death in 1641.

GALILEO GALILEI (1564–1642)

Galileo Galilei was born at Pisa, Italy, and became one of the greatest scientists of all time. He developed the use of a pendulum to record time and he perfected a refracting telescope, using it to discover the four moons of Jupiter in 1610. He also discovered that Earth's moon reflects the light of the sun. In later life he was imprisoned for acknowledging Copernicus's theory that the sun, not the Earth, was at the centre of our Solar System.

THE LONG AND SHORT PARLIAMENTS

Charles's rule without Parliament became increasingly difficult as time went on. In 1637 he forced the English Prayer Book onto Scotland, which led to open rebellion. Unable to contain the revolt, Charles was forced to recall Parliament three years later. The first attempt was short-lived and lasted only three weeks (known as the 'Short Parliament'). Charles quarrelled with Parliament again, eventually resulting in civil war. Parliament was recalled again, this time lasting until 1660 (known as the 'Long Parliament'). Between 1649-60 England was run by Parliament as a republic.

HENRIETTA MARIA

Charles married Henrietta Maria, daughter of the French king, Henry IV, in 1625 shortly after acceding to the throne. She was only 16 years old and of slightly gawky appearance and the two were not immediately attracted to one another. After 1628 when the king's favourite, the Duke of Buckingham, was assassinated, Charles turned to her for comfort and they became a devoted couple. After Charles's execution in 1649 Henrietta returned to France.

EXECUTION

Charles remains the only British monarch to have been formally charged with treason and executed. Parliament took the unprecedented step of trying the king for waging war against his own people, though Charles refused to acknowledge the legality of the court or to justify his actions. The trial began on 20th January 1649 and lasted just one week. Found guilty, he was executed three days later, on 30th January, by beheading, to a very mixed reaction from the populace.

1625	1627	1629	a Dutch artist, to settle	1640
James's second son succeeds to the throne as Charles I.	England declares war on France once again.	Charles dissolves Parliament again, rules without them until 1640.	in England and become court painter.	Short Parliament summoned.
1626	1628	1632	1637	1640
Charles dissolves Parliament.	The Petition of Right is presented to the king.	Charles invites Van Dyck,	Charles tries to force English prayer book onto Scots.	Long Parliament Summoned; lasts until 1660

🏛 ARCHITECTURE   📖 ARTS & LITERATURE   ⚑ EXPLORATION   💣 FAMOUS BATTLES

CHARLES I

BORN 1600 • ACCEDED 1625 • EXECUTED 1649

harles I was another who was not born to be king and did not expect to rule, only inheriting the crown following the death of his elder brother, Henry, in 1612. A slight man of diminutive stature, he also had a slight stammer, reflecting his shyness and lack of self-confidence. He was an intelligent man and a great patron of the arts who carried a dignified air, far removed from the appalling personal manners of his father.

SPECIAL PRIVILEGE

Like his father, James I, Charles believed uncompromisingly in the 'Divine Right of Kings'. Although a medieval doctrine, the power of the monarchy had been considerably reduced in England since those times with the growth in power of Parliament. Not so in Scotland, however, the Stuarts' ancestral homeland, where kings believed they ruled with divine grace and were answerable only to God, not to their fellow men.

CHARLES DISSOLVES PARLIAMENT

Charles's belief in his 'divine' right to rule unhindered frequently brought him into conflict with Parliament. Following the death of his favourite George Villiers, Duke of Buckingham, Charles decided to dissolve Parliament, ruling on his own for 11 years, between 1629-40 using the Court of the Star Chamber and the Court of High Commission to support his actions and dismiss any opposition.

FAMILY MAN

Although a shy man by nature, Charles was very much aware of his responsibilities as king and performed his duties with quiet dignity. He often overcompensated for his shyness, which was seen by many as haughty arrogance. Basically a family man, he was happiest when surrounded by his wife and children (of which he had nine).

1641 The Court of the Star Chamber abolished.	**1642** Charles tries unsuccessfully to arrest five members of Parliament.	War between Charles and Parliament.	**1644** Royalists defeated at Battle of Marston Moor.	him up to Cromwell.
1641 Catholic revolt in Ireland; many Protestants massacred.	**1642** Outbreak of Civil	**1642** Royalists defeat Parliament at Battle of Edgehill.	**1646** Charles surrenders to Scots, but they give	**1649** Civil War ends. **1649** Charles arrested, tried and executed.

GOVERNMENT   HEALTH & MEDICINE   JUSTICE   RELIGION   SCIENCE

THE CIVIL WAR
(1642–1649)

Although England had frequently witnessed civil wars, these were mostly local and regional. The Civil War of 1642-49 was the first time the entire country had ranged itself into two distinct factions between king and Parliament, and the first time since the Battle of Bosworth in 1485 that fellow Englishmen had taken up arms against one another. The Stuart notion of ruling by divine right was certain to lead to conflict with Parliament, which came to a head in 1642 when Charles tried to arrest five members of Parliament. The Civil War was a turning point in our constitutional history, for even though the monarchy was restored in 1660 following a brief period as a republic, it was never again able to wield such power and became much more accountable.

PRINCE RUPERT

Prince Rupert was the German-born nephew of Charles I who came to his uncle's aid in 1642 at the age of 23. A talented young man of science, he quickly became also an outstanding military commander. His speciality was lightning cavalry charges, using lightly armed soldiers, who attacked the ill-equipped and inexperienced Parliamentary troops at full gallop, making best use of the element of surprise.

CAVALIERS

The Royalist forces were known as Cavaliers and were usually clothed in resplendent uniforms based on court dress of the day, including knee-length leather boots, tunics and flamboyant hats complete with plumes.

ROUNDHEADS

The Parliamentarians were less well-equipped, especially in the early years of the war. Their uniforms were much simpler and consisted of leather over-tunics, metal helmets and, later, metal breastplates.

ARCHITECTURE   ARTS & LITERATURE   EXPLORATION   FAMOUS BATTLES

DEATH WARRANT

At his trial, Charles refused to acknowledge the court and refused to plead. He wore a black suit and remained eloquent and dignified throughout the proceedings. His death warrant (shown here) was signed by 59 chosen republicans and stated that he should be executed by beheading. When the monarchy was restored in 1660 most of the signatories fled abroad, or escaped execution themselves by repenting their actions, but 10 of the regicides who refused to repent were executed for treason.

NEW MODEL ARMY

In February 1645 Parliament created a revolutionary new military system, the New Model Army. Nationally organized and regularly paid, it was the basis of the armed services today. Commanding officers were promoted to rank based on their abilities rather than on their social standing. Sir Thomas Fairfax was commander of the new army, with Oliver Cromwell, a leading figure in the Parliamentary cause, the Lieutenant-General. Well drilled and disciplined, Cromwell personally oversaw the army's rigorous training programme.

A PRISONER IN CARISBROOKE CASTLE

In 1646 Charles surrendered to the Scots, expecting compassion, but they handed him over to Cromwell. He escaped, briefly, but was recaptured and imprisoned in Carisbrooke Castle, on the Isle of Wight, where he remained for a year.

BATTLE OF EDGEHILL

The Battle of Edgehill was the first major conflict of the Civil War. Fought on a hill in the Cotswolds, both sides were evenly matched, consisting of about 12,000 men each, and both lost about 2,500 by the end of the day, over half through desertion. It was not a pitched battle and both sides seemed reluctant to fight their fellow Englishmen, but it marked the beginning of seven years of bloody conflict. Both sides claimed victory, but the Royalist forces had the better of the day, though they failed to capitalize on their advantage.

BATTLE OF MARSTON MOOR

The early years of the war belonged to the Royalists, who at one stage looked like winning, under the daring leadership of Prince Rupert. The turning point came in 1644, at the Battle of Marston Moor. Cromwell won a resounding victory, earning Rupert's respect in his epitaph when he called the Parliamentarians 'ironsides'.

BATTLE OF NASEBY

Cromwell's New Model Army was put to the test at the Battle of Naseby in June 1645. The Parliamentary army, at 15,000 strong, was twice the size of the Royalist force and easily won the day. One of the most decisive victories of the campaign, it effectively marked the end of the Civil War. Charles was captured and imprisoned the following year and although the war dragged on until 1649, the Royalists were a spent force after the battle.

GOVERNMENT   HEALTH & MEDICINE   JUSTICE   RELIGION   SCIENCE

THE COMMONWEALTH
(1649–1660)

Britain's only brush with republicanism was short-lived. The dominant figure throughout the Civil War, and later the Commonwealth, was Oliver Cromwell (see pages 12-13) and, although he devised a new, and in many ways fairer system of government, it was never fully democratic and it disintegrated when he died. Although a brilliant leader, the strength of his leadership lay in his personal qualities and not in the reforms he introduced. His successor, his son Richard, proved an inept politician and within two years of Oliver Cromwell's death, Parliament recalled the monarchy.

CHARLES II GOES INTO EXILE

Following the defeat of the Scots at the Battle of Dunbar, (see bottom right) Charles II led another rebellious Scottish force against Cromwell at the Battle of Worcester in 1651, but he was defeated and afterwards forced into exile, first to France and then to Holland.

THE DUTCH WARS

As a direct result of the commercial rivalry caused by the Navigation Act, the first of a series of three wars between England and Holland broke out between 1652-4. England's military and naval prowess increased significantly in the early years of the Commonwealth under Cromwell's leadership and the Dutch fleet was routed by Robert Blake.

THE RUMP PARLIAMENT

The 'Rump Parliament' was a derisive name given to the 'Long Parliament'. It had sat for 13 years and many of its members had deserted leaving, by 1653, fewer than 60 of its original 490 members. During the Civil War it was Cromwell's army that had won the day, not Parliament, which in his eyes seemed as corrupt as the monarchy itself. In 1653 he dismissed the Rump Parliament and ruled instead with the army.

1649 Council of State appoints Oliver Cromwell as Chairman to rule country.	declared a republic. **1649** Irish rebels, loyal to Charles, defeated at Battles of Wexford and Drogheda.	**1650** Scots royalists defeated at Battle of Dunbar.	**1651** Charles II claims the throne, but is defeated by Cromwell at Worcester and forced into exile.	protect English shipping. **1653** Rump Parliament dismissed by Cromwell.
1649 England is		**1650** Vacuum pump invented.	**1651** Navigation Act passed to	**1653** Cromwell declared Lord

🏛 ARCHITECTURE   📖 ARTS & LITERATURE   📜 EXPLORATION   ⚫ FAMOUS BATTLES

ENGLAND DECLARED A REPUBLIC

The period known as the Commonwealth can roughly be divided into two phases. The first, known as the Republic, spanned the period 1649–53, where Cromwell attempted to govern within the existing parliamentary structure, but drastic reforms were needed if the monarchy were to be replaced with a sustainable form of government. The second period was known as the Protectorate (see below).

THE PROTECTORATE

The second period of the Commonwealth was known as the Protectorate and lasted from 1653–9. When Cromwell dismissed the Long Parliament in 1653 he effectively set himself up as leader of a dictatorship, assuming the title Lord Protector of England. He ruled with the aid of his New Model Army and formed a new Parliament which, in 1657, offered him the monarchy, but he refused. In all, three Protectorate Parliaments were called by Cromwell, and each was dismissed by him as it failed to live up to his ideals. When Cromwell died in 1658 his son Richard became Lord Protector, but he lacked his father's qualities and was dismissed by Parliament in 1660 when they invited Charles II to return as king.

COUNCIL OF STATE

The remaining members of the Long Parliament, who had called for Charles I's execution, formed a Council of State in 1649 with Oliver Cromwell as chairman. Many of the members were interested only in their own needs and obstructed many of Cromwell's parliamentary reforms, which prompted Cromwell to rule as dictator.

🔘 SIEGE OF DROGHEDA

Irish and Scots royalists led a combined rebellion against Parliament following Charles I's execution, though in the case of the Irish this was seen more as a means of removing English rule from Ireland than in supporting Charles II's cause. Cromwell defeated the Irish at Wexford and at the Siege of Drogheda in 1649.

📜 NAVIGATION ACT

In 1651 the Navigation Act was passed, which gave English merchant ships a monopoly over foreign imports and exports from English ports. This had the effect of bolstering the English economy and led directly to conflict with Holland.

🔘 BATTLE OF DUNBAR

Following the execution of Charles I his son, Charles II, was proclaimed king by the Scots, despite their having betrayed his father by handing him over to Parliament. Cromwell's answer was swift and decisive. He defeated the Scots at the Battle of Dunbar in 1650.

Protector of England.
1654
First Protectorate
Parliament called.
1655
Cromwell dismisses

Parliament and rules with
his army, headed by 11
Major-Generals.
1655
English take Jamaica
from the Spanish.

1657
Cromwell offered the
throne, but refuses.
1658
Third Protectorate
Parliament dismissed

by Cromwell.
1658
Oliver Cromwell dies.
1658
Oliver's son, Richard
Cromwell, becomes

Lord Protector.
1660
Restoration of
the monarchy
recommended by the
new Parliament.

📕 GOVERNMENT   🥣 HEALTH & MEDICINE   ⚖️ JUSTICE   ✝️ RELIGION   📋 SCIENCE

OFFERED THE CROWN

Cromwell was offered the crown of England by the Protectorate Parliament in 1657. His attempts to reform government failed and he had to rely more and more on military force, which caused further divisions. By inviting him to become king, Parliament thought the divided country might unite behind a common cause, but Cromwell refused, saying that he was against the principle of hereditary rule. His own generals were against the idea also and threatened revolt if he accepted the crown.

OLIVER CROMWELL
(Lord Protector)

BORN 1599 • APPOINTED CHAIRMAN OF COUNCIL OF STATE 1649
APPOINTED LORD PROTECTOR 1653 • DIED 1658

liver Cromwell was born in 1599, the son of a wealthy Huntingdonshire squire. He was tall, though not handsome, and of somewhat slovenly appearance. He entered politics at the age of 29 but had a remarkably uneventful career until the outbreak of the Civil War. A self-taught soldier who learnt his tactical skills by reading military accounts, he led a cavalry unit in East Anglia at the outset of the war.

He was a charismatic man who quickly rose through the ranks by showing his military prowess and by 1644 he was appointed Lieutenant-General for all the Parliamentary armies and came to be regarded as one of the finest commanders in Europe.

JAMAICA CAPTURED

While many of his fellow countrymen viewed Cromwell with suspicion and even hatred because of the harsh laws he imposed, those abroad regarded him with grudging respect and admiration. His reorganization of the armed services gave him great prestige in Europe. The Dutch were routed at sea and many of the Spanish dominions were attacked, including Jamaica, which was taken in 1655.

🏛 ARCHITECTURE   📖 ARTS & LITERATURE   🏳 EXPLORATION   🔥 FAMOUS BATTLES

LORD PROTECTOR OF ENGLAND

When he realised that Parliament did not entirely support his reforms, Cromwell decided to go it alone and in 1653 declared himself Lord Protector of England. Despite his democratic and religious ideals, he never sought open and free elections for fear of losing, because many of his policies were unpopular. Instead, he justified his dictatorial stance by claiming that he acted in the name of God for the people's best interests; ironically, not too dissimilar to the Stuart-held belief of the 'Divine Right of Kings'!

DEVOUTLY RELIGIOUS

Cromwell was a devoutly religious man, tolerant of most religious views (except Catholicism) and adopted a Puritan lifestyle although, contrary to popular view, his own beliefs were not extreme and he was not averse to pleasure seeking, in moderation. He believed passionately in his mission to remove the tyrant monarchy from Britain and replace it with a fairer system of government and felt that in so doing he was being guided by God's hand.

RESTORATION OF THE MONARCHY

The act of removing what he saw as a tyrannical monarchy proved an easier task than finding a suitable system of government to replace it. Cromwell had largely won the Civil War with his New Model Army, with little assistance from Parliament, and when he later came to introduce radical reforms he discovered that Parliament was just as corrupt as the monarchy had ever been. Consequently, he introduced stricter and stricter methods to control the country, which had the effect of stifling the population and turned many people against the idea of a republic. Within two years of his death, Parliament itself invited Charles II to return from exile as king. Certain conditions were imposed on his restoration to prevent royal excesses occurring again, but by and large the return of the monarchy was welcomed.

PURITAN LIFESTYLE

Cromwell had a vision to reform corruption in society, not just in removing a self-indulgent monarchy, but in restoring the people to a more righteous way of life. He followed a Puritan lifestyle and rejected many of the old religious ways, which he saw as popish. Festivals such as Christmas and May Day were abolished, drinking and swearing were forbidden, as was profaning the Sabbath, and everyone was required to attend church. He was not averse to enjoyment, but its excesses were strictly controlled, making him very unpopular with the people.

📖 JOHN MILTON

John Milton, born in 1608, represented the spirit of the age in his deeply religious poetry. A devout Puritan, he became the Commonwealth's semi-official spokesman in 1649 but, like Cromwell himself, he saw all his dreams and ideals shattered in his lifetime. The so-called 'English Revolution' had come to nothing. His most famous works, 'Paradise Lost' and 'Paradise Regained', express his disillusionment with the politics of the day. He went blind at the age of 44 and died in 1674.

📜 **GOVERNMENT**   🥄 **HEALTH & MEDICINE**   ⚖️ **JUSTICE**   ✝ **RELIGION**   🧪 **SCIENCE**

CHARLES II

BORN 1630 • ACCEDED 1660 • DIED 1685

*f*ollowing the execution of his father, Charles I, in 1649 and his unsuccessful attempts to ascend the throne, Charles was forced into exile, initially to France, but afterwards to Germany and Holland. Although technically still king, Charles had little money and for 11 years lived a frugal existence. When Oliver Cromwell died in 1658 the Commonwealth began to collapse. To avert another civil war, Parliament asked the exiled king to return to England. He arrived in London on 29th May 1660, on his 30th birthday. Cromwell's body was exhumed and hanged at Tyburn, but otherwise the Restoration passed without further recriminations.

CHARLES II

The restoration of Charles II was greeted with wild enthusiasm by a population that had suffered considerable repression under Puritan rule. Although Charles acknowledged having 14 illegitimate children, he had none by his wife. On his death the throne passed to his brother, James.

FLIGHT FOR FREEDOM

After the execution of his father, Charles led a revolt against Parliament. He lost to Cromwell at the Battle of Worcester in 1651 and fled to France.

THE NAVAL COLLEGE

The royal palace of Placentia, that formerly stood at Greenwich, was rebuilt by Charles II to designs by Sir Christopher Wren. The magnificent buildings were later converted for use as a naval hospital, college and maritime museum.

1660
Charles II asked to return to England as king.

1660
Samuel Pepys begins writing his diaries.

1661
First Parliament of Charles's reign called.

1661
Corporation Act prevents Nonconformists

from holding governmental posts.

1662
Act of Uniformity makes Puritans accept Anglican Church.

1662
Royal Society given royal charter.

1665/7
War breaks out with Holland, leads to

humiliating naval defeat for English at Chatham.

1665
Extensive outbreak of the plague, especially in London.

🏛 ARCHITECTURE   📖 ARTS & LITERATURE   ⚐ EXPLORATION   💣 FAMOUS BATTLES

THE DUTCH WARS

There were three separate wars with Holland during the 17th century, one during the Commonwealth and two during Charles's reign. In 1667 the English suffered a humiliating defeat when the Dutch sailed up the River Medway and laid waste the fleet anchored at Chatham Dockyard, in Kent.

A MERRY MONARCH

When in 1660 Charles was invited to become king, as part of the bargain he had to marry Catherine of Braganza, from Portugal. It was a loveless marriage and Charles, who was tall and handsome, took an estimated 17 mistresses. The most notable of these was Nell Gwynne, whom he openly courted and who is believed to have given him two sons. Charles was a popular figure who delighted in pleasurable pursuits, such as gambling, hunting and boating.

✛ A CHANGE OF MIND

Charles II was a flamboyant character who resented the stifling attitudes of the church, particularly after the puritanical zeal of Oliver Cromwell's time. On his deathbed in 1685 he reverted to Catholicism.

⬭ THE ROYAL SOCIETY

From 1645 a group of people, interested in scientific discovery, began meeting on a regular basis in Oxford and London. Charles was himself very interested in science and in 1662 granted them a charter, marking the founding of the Royal Society.

📜 THE 'WHIGS' & 'TORIES'

The names of the political parties Whigs (Liberals) and Tories (Conservatives) have their origins in the Civil War. The Whigs, founded by Lord Shaftesbury, were pro-Parliament, while the Tories supported the monarchy. The names were first used in 1679.

SIR CHRISTOPHER WREN

Sir Christopher Wren was born in 1632 and by the age of 29 was already Professor of Astronomy at Oxford. He was a founder member of the Royal Society and was interested in all aspects of science. He came late to architecture, when he was asked to design the Sheldonian Theatre at Oxford. He went on to design many churches and public buildings in the Classical style. In 1666 he submitted a plan to build a dome for the medieval St. Paul's Cathedral, London. When the cathedral burnt down in the Great Fire, he was asked to design a replacement cathedral. The result was the magnificent cathedral we see today. Begun in 1675 it was completed in 1710. Wren died in 1723 aged 91.

1666
Great Fire of London breaks out.
1666
Isaac Newton discovers the solar spectrum.

1670
Charles signs Treaty of Dover and agrees in secret to restore Catholicism to England.
1670
Hudson Bay Company

founded for fur trading in North America.
1673
Test Act prevents Catholics from holding government office.

1678
The Popish Plot, supposedly a Catholic plot to assassinate the king.
1683
Rye House Plot; a further

attempt to assassinate Charles.
1685
Charles converts to Catholicism on his deathbed.

📜 GOVERNMENT   ⚱ HEALTH & MEDICINE   ⚖ JUSTICE   ✛ RELIGION   ⬭ SCIENCE

HOW THE FIRE STARTED

The fire started in the premises of Thomas Farriner, in Pudding Lane, at about midnight on Saturday 1st September 1666. Farriner was a baker and, according to a statement he gave later, he checked his ovens before retiring to bed. He was awakened a few hours later by smoke and fled to nearby premises. His own housemaid was the fire's first victim. Several nearby warehouses containing pitch aided the spread of the fire, assisted by a fanning wind. The site of the fire is marked by a monument in Pudding Lane, designed by Sir Christopher Wren.

FIGHTING THE FIRE

Defences against the fire were woefully inadequate and consisted principally of leather buckets and hand-squirts (a kind of syphon) with people forming human bucket chains. With no running water supplies, water had to be fetched from the river or from wells. There was no organized fire service and the only effective remedy was to destroy houses in the path of the fire to create fire-breaks. The fire eventually burnt itself out on 6th September when the wind changed direction.

THE DAMAGE CAUSED

Many of the buildings of London were constructed of timber and thatch and the fire quickly spread out of control through the narrow streets. It burnt for nearly five days, destroying old St. Paul's Cathedral, 88 churches and about 13,200 houses and other buildings in its wake, making an estimated 100,000 people homeless, though miraculously only nine people died.

EXTENT OF THE BLAZE

The map on the left shows the extent of the blaze. Over four-fifths of the City of London, within the old city walls, was destroyed, covering an area in excess of 430 acres.

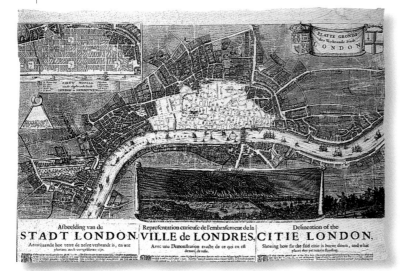

🏛 ARCHITECTURE   📖 ARTS & LITERATURE   ⚑ EXPLORATION   ● FAMOUS BATTLES

FIRE & PLAGUE
(1665–66)

etween June 1665 and September 1666 London suffered two quite catastrophic disasters. The first of these was a serious outbreak of the plague followed, a year later, by the most devastating fire this country has ever witnessed. Many Puritans saw it as divine retribution following the Restoration of the monarchy. Ironically, although the outbreak of plague continued a while longer, the fire stemmed the worst of its ravages. Although localised outbreaks occurred at intervals for the next two centuries, this was the last major epidemic of plague in England.

OUTBREAK OF PLAGUE

The plague first appeared in Britain in the mid-14th century (though similar diseases may have been around since Saxon times), brought here from the Middle East by flea-infected rats aboard merchant ships. During that outbreak it is estimated between ⅓ and ⅕ of the population died. It was principally a disease of the poor, spread by rats in the insanitary living conditions of the time, but no-one was immune. The outbreak of 1665–6, known as the Great Plague, was one of many epidemics that occurred periodically in Britain from the 14th to the 19th centuries and ranks as one of the worst, killing an estimated 100,000 people in London alone. It was more prevalent in towns and many of the rich, including Charles II, moved to country retreats until the epidemic subsided.

REBUILDING LONDON

Charles II himself, and his brother James, are said to have assisted in fighting the fire and the king rode amongst the homeless a few days later to quash rumours that the fire had been started deliberately by England's enemies. Charles saw the opportunity of rebuilding the centre of London to a grand new design and commissioned Christopher Wren to design a new capital. The plans he submitted were never fully carried out, but he was responsible for many new buildings, including a new St. Paul's Cathedral and over 50 other churches.

WHAT IS THE PLAGUE?

The plague is a severe infectious fever caused by the bacterium 'Pasteurella pestis' and is transmitted to humans, from rats, by their fleas. There are two forms: bubonic and pneumonic plague. The symptoms of bubonic plague are fever, followed by swollen lymph nodes in the neck, armpits and groin. Dark blotches, caused by internal bleeding, are one reason for its other name, the 'Black Death'. Over half of all victims in the 17th century died within five days. The more serious pneumonic plague infected the lungs and was usually 100% fatal. Although rare, the plague still exists in certain hot countries, but can normally be cured with strong antibiotics.

EFFECTS OF THE PLAGUE

Scarcely a family in the land was unaffected by the plague. One of the principal effects of the disease was the obvious decimation of the population but ironically, for those who survived, living conditions temporarily improved. Because of the scarcity of labour, particularly after the major epidemics, those who survived were able to command higher wages, until the authorities legislated against it.

GOVERNMENT   HEALTH & MEDICINE   JUSTICE   RELIGION   SCIENCE

◈ BATTLE OF SEDGMOOR

The Battle of Sedgmoor, fought on 6th July 1685, was the last land battle to be fought in England. It was fought between the Duke of Monmouth who, as Charles II's illegitimate son, claimed the throne, and James II's army. The battle was short-lived and lasted only about four hours. Monmouth's men were hopelessly outnumbered and outmanoeuvred and the royal troops easily won the day.

✟ DECLARATION OF INDULGENCE

James openly encouraged the re-introduction of Catholic rites and institutions in religious and court life, replacing many Protestant government officers with Catholic favourites. In 1688 he introduced the Declaration of Indulgence, which suspended all laws against Catholics and Non-Conformists.

✟ RESTORATION OF CATHOLICISM

James converted to Catholicism in the 1660s, much to the disapproval of Parliament, who removed him from high office and tried, unsuccessfully, to prevent his succession to the throne. He declared from the outset that he intended to restore Catholicism as the main religion of Britain. To help him achieve this he increased the standing army from 6,000 to 30,000, replacing many of the Protestant officers with Catholics.

◉ SIR ISAAC NEWTON

The Stuart age was a period of great advances in science. One of the greatest scientists of the day was Sir Isaac Newton (1642-1727) who made a major contribution to our understanding of mathematics and physics, including the law of gravity. He also developed the reflecting telescope.

Elizabeth Gaunt was burnt for harbouring rebels after the battle of Sedgmoor.

'THE GLORIOUS REVOLUTION'

In 1688 Parliament invited William of Orange, ruler of Holland and James's son-in-law, to restore liberties to England. He landed at Brixham, in Devon, on 5th November 1688, with an invasion force. Although William was not a popular figure, James II had little support himself and the Dutchman was able to march on London and force the king's deposition in a virtually bloodless coup.

DUKE OF MONMOUTH

James, Duke of Monmouth, was the illegitimate son of Charles II and within a few months of James II's accession he led a Protestant rebellion against the Catholic king in a bid for the throne. He was a vain, ambitious man who was used by the king's political adversaries in an attempt to remove him from the throne. The plan was ill-conceived and badly executed, however, resulting in Monmouth's defeat at the Battle of Sedgmoor in Somerset in 1685 and his execution shortly after.

PROTESTANT REFUGEES

In 1682, in France, over 60,000 Protestants had been forcibly converted to Catholicism followed, in 1685, by the revocation of the Edict of Nantes, which no longer made it possible for Protestants to practise their religion freely. Many Protestant refugees fled France and settled in England, particularly on the east coast, bringing their crafts and skills with them. They were especially adept in the art of clothmaking and greatly influenced the trade in this country.

1685	Charles II, leads rebellion	1685	standing army of over	1686
Charles's brother succeeds	*against James.*	*Edict of Nantes is revoked*	*12,000 to intimidate the*	*Dominion of New*
to the throne as James II.	**1685**	*in France; many Huguenot*	*inhabitants of London.*	*England established.*
1685	*Duke of Monmouth*	*refugees flee to England.*	**1686**	**1687**
Duke of Monmouth the	*defeated at Battle of*	**1686**	*James attempts to restore*	*Isaac Newton publishes*
illegitimate son of	*Sedgmoor, later executed.*	*James sets up a*	*Catholicism to England.*	*his first major work*

🏛 ARCHITECTURE   📖 ARTS & LITERATURE   ⚐ EXPLORATION   ◈ FAMOUS BATTLES

JAMES II

BORN 1633 • ACCEDED 1685 • DEPOSED 1688 • DIED 1701

ike all the Stuarts, James was a proud, haughty man, who believed strongly in the doctrine of the Divine Right of Kings. He was the second son of Charles I and acceded on the death of his brother, Charles II, who had no legitimate children to inherit the throne. He spent much of his early life in government office and was made Lord High Admiral, serving in the Dutch wars, but aroused considerable opposition from Parliament because of his strong Catholic views. Although tall, handsome and by all accounts well-mannered, because of his arrogance he never won the popular support of his people.

JAMES ABDICATES

When faced with the choice of accepting Parliament's demands or deposition, James refused to compromise his ideals and chose abdication. He was deposed on 23rd December 1688 and forced into exile in France, where he died in 1701, it is believed from syphilis.

TRIAL OF THE SEVEN BISHOPS

As part of his drive towards Catholicism, James ordered all Protestant clergy to read the Declaration of Indulgence out loud in their churches. There was much opposition and many refused. Sancroft, Archbishop of Canterbury, and six other bishops petitioned James to withdraw the order but he had them arrested for seditious libel. They were sent for trial at Westminster, but were acquitted, amidst much jubilation.

JUDGE JEFFREYS & THE BLOODY ASSIZES

Following the Duke of Monmouth's ill-fated attempt to seize the crown, the remaining rebels were put on trial by the notorious Judge Jeffreys. At 40 Jeffreys became the youngest Lord Chancellor and he soon acquired a reputation as being the most brutal. The series of trials against the rebels soon degenerated into a farce as Jeffreys bullied and intimidated the witnesses. He executed over 300 of the Protestant rebels and transported about 1,000 more to the colonies. The infamous trials came to be known as the 'Bloody Assizes'.

on mathematics.
1688
Declaration of Indulgence repeals all anti-Catholic and anti-Non-Conformist laws.

1688
James's second wife, Mary of Modena, gives birth to a son, James Edward, who becomes his favoured Catholic heir.

1688
Trial of the Seven Bishops for seditious libel.
1688
William of Orange, the Dutch ruler, is

invited to accept the throne of England.
1688
The Glorious Revolution; William lands in England and seizes

the throne, virtually unopposed.
1688
James is forced to abdicate and flee to France in exile.

GOVERNMENT   HEALTH & MEDICINE   JUSTICE   RELIGION   SCIENCE

HOW WE GOT OUR PARLIAMENT

oday we live in a democracy (from the Greek words 'demos', meaning people, and 'kratos', meaning power), governed by an elected body of representatives known as Members of Parliament. Britain prides itself in having one of the fairest systems of government in the world, but things were not always so. The change from an absolute monarchy to a constitutional monarchy, where the king or queen is merely a figurehead, was a slow process. The Parliament we have today is the result of many centuries of struggle by right-minded people who felt we should all have a say in how our country is governed and many lost their lives in the process.

MAGNA CARTA

The first milestone in British constitutional history was when the barons forced King John to sign Magna Carta (or Great Charter) in 1215. The original version contained 63 clauses that curbed absolute royal power. Although largely ignored by subsequent monarchs, it formed the corner-stone of the governmental reforms that followed in later centuries.

SIMON DE MONTFORT

Known as the 'Father of English Parliament', Simon de Montfort determined to make government less exclusive and more accountable by reducing the power of the monarchy. He called the first open English Parliament in 1265, but met his death at the hands of the King's Court (as shown here).

THE SAXON WITAN

Saxon kings ruled with a council of personally selected advisers known as the Witan, who made all the national decisions. Beneath that were three separate tiers of local government, roughly corresponding to the shire (or county), town and parish councils still in existence today, known as moot councils, though few elements of society were eligible to sit on the councils.

THE FEUDAL SYSTEM

In many respects the Saxon system of government was fairer than the feudal system that followed it. Introduced by the Normans after the Conquest of 1066 the king ruled with absolute power. The moot councils were retained, but they merely acted as the king's agents. Under the feudal system, all land ultimately belonged to the crown, which was then let to various levels of sub-tenants in return for military service.

EDWARD I'S MODEL PARLIAMENT

Edward I agreed, in principle, with Simon de Montfort's call for government reforms. In 1295 he called the first democratically elected (at least partially) Parliament known as the 'Model Parliament', comprising lords, clergy, knights and elected representatives from the community, sitting in two houses, the Lords and the Commons.

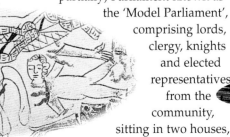

🏛 ARCHITECTURE　📖 ARTS & LITERATURE　🏴 EXPLORATION　🖊 FAMOUS BATTLES

PARTY POLITICS

The ongoing feud between king and Parliament finally came to a head in the Civil War of 1642-49 (Charles is shown, attempting to arrest 5 members of the Houses of Parliament). Until then, although the monarchy ruled with Parliament, the king could still call or dismiss a parliament at will. The beginnings of the party system of politics emerged at this time.

THE COMMONWEALTH

The Commonwealth (1649-60) was the only period in our history when Parliament ruled as a republic, without a monarchy (see pages 10-11).

BILL OF RIGHTS

Introduced in 1689, the Bill of Rights is usually seen as the second most important constitutional reform after Magna Carta. Its main clauses were that no Catholic could become the ruling monarch and taxes and laws could only be implemented with parliamentary consent.

THE PEOPLE'S CHARTER

In 1838 the People's Charter was issued by a group of people, known as the Chartists, campaigning for political reform. Its main clauses called for the right to vote for everyone, the right for anyone to seek election, secret ballots and equal representation. Although not fully realised until as late as 1944, the Charter forms the basis of our modern constitution.

REFORM ACT OF 1832

Prior to 1832 only certain classes of people were allowed to vote, namely property owners and landowners. The first Reform Act of that year greatly extended the vote and ensured a fairer distribution of parliamentary seats based on population. Subsequent acts in 1867 and 1884 further reformed the system.

SECRET BALLOT

In 1872 the Secret Ballot was introduced into the electoral system to eliminate vote rigging and possible recriminations. Surprisingly, the vote was not extended to all women of 21 and over until 1928.

THE HOUSES OF PARLIAMENT

The present Houses of Parliament were completed in 1867 to designs by Pugin and Barry after the old Palace of Westminster burnt down in 1834. Formerly, Parliament met in St. Stephen's Chapel (known as Parliament House), given to the Commons by Edward VI and once part of the royal palace.

GOVERNMENT   HEALTH & MEDICINE   JUSTICE   RELIGION   SCIENCE

WILLIAM III
& MARY II

WILLIAM III BORN 1650 • ACCEDED 1689 • DIED 1702
MARY II BORN 1662 • ACCEDED 1689 • DIED 1694

*U*ntil 1688, the Protestant Mary was heir to the throne, but when James II's second wife, Mary of Modena, gave birth to a son in that year, succession passed to him. Mary, among many others, doubted the legitimacy of this baby, whom James declared would be brought up a Catholic, which was against Parliament's wishes and prompted the king's deposition later the same year. In 1677 Mary married William of Orange (the name given to the Dutch royal family) who was the son of William of Nassau and Mary Stuart. William was a man of slight build and was never very popular with the English, unlike Mary, who was much liked. She died at the premature age of 32, from smallpox.

INVITATION TO THE ENGLISH THRONE

To prevent the line of succession passing into Catholic hands and thus consolidating James II's anti-Protestant stand, in 1688 Parliament invited the Dutch ruler William of Orange to England, initially to restore lost liberties under James's rule and ultimately, if the king refused to accept the conditions laid down by Parliament, to depose James and rule in his place. William accepted, but Parliament imposed certain conditions, namely that he ruled jointly with James's eldest daughter Mary (whom William had married 12 years before) and that he accept a number of constitutional restraints on royal power. William accepted the conditions, though he had little interest in England, using this situation simply to strengthen Holland's position against France.

A RIDING ACCIDENT

William III was a slightly-built man with a passion for riding and hunting. He was an accomplished horseman, taking part in several military campaigns, and his death as a result of a riding accident in 1702 came as a great surprise.

BANK OF ENGLAND FOUNDED

The Bank of England was founded in 1694, initially to fund William's wars against France, but it later served as a means of securing government credit in peacetime. The bank moved to its present site in Threadneedle Street in 1734.

1689
Parliament issues the Declaration of Right detailing the case against James II.

1689
William of Orange is invited to rule, jointly, with his wife Mary II, James's daughter.
1689
Toleration Act allows

freedom of worship.
1689
First Mutiny Bill abolishes standing armies without permission by Parliament.

1689
Scottish-led Catholic rebellion against William crushed.
1689
Bill of Rights determines

future succession to the throne.
1689
James II defeated at Siege of Londonderry, in Ireland.

🏛 ARCHITECTURE   📖 ARTS & LITERATURE   🏳 EXPLORATION   🛢 FAMOUS BATTLES

LOYALTY REWARDED

Henry Sidney, of Penshurst Place, in Kent was one of the leading Whigs of the day who supported James II's deposition and was one of those who invited William of Orange to take the throne. His reward was in being created Earl of Romney, as detailed in the Patent, shown left.

MUTINY BILL

One of the charges brought against James II by Parliament, which added to his unpopularity, was his raising of a massive standing army during peacetime. To prevent such a situation arising again the Mutiny Bill was passed in 1689 which forbade the raising of a standing army without parliamentary approval.

SCOTTISH REBELLION

When Charles II was restored to the throne in 1660 Scotland was once again accepted as a separate kingdom. When William III came to the throne, however, the Scots saw this independence threatened and many rebelled against his usurpation of the throne, for James II came from the royal Scottish family of Stuart. The rebellion was put down later in 1689 and the Scots made to swear an oath of allegiance to William.

GLENCOE MASSACRE

Pockets of resistance continued to exist in Scotland long after the main rebellion against William's rule was put down. A series of localised clan wars broke out, which came to a head in 1692 at the Massacre of Glencoe. Glencoe, a remote valley in the Highlands, was the family home of the Macdonalds. Under the orders of William, the rival clan of Campbell massacred many of the Macdonalds while they slept and so put down the rebellion once and for all.

WAR OF SPANISH SUCCESSION

In 1700 Charles II of Spain died without leaving an heir. The Spanish empire, which included part of the Netherlands (an area roughly corresponding to the modern state of Belgium) was settled upon Louis XIV's grandson, Duke Philip of Anjou. Louis also recognised James II's son as legitimate heir to the English throne. To prevent France from acquiring the Spanish domains, in 1701 William entered into an alliance with Holland and Austria, thus beginning the War of Spanish Succession.

✝ TOLERATION ACT

In 1689 the Toleration Act was passed which assured the freedom for all to worship as they chose, without fear of recrimination.

⚫ BATTLE OF THE BOYNE

Following James II's deposition by William of Orange, the Irish Catholics sided with James in a rebellion. The Irish Protestants, who had mostly settled around Ulster, sided with William. James first tried , unsuccessfully, to besiege Londonderry and then moved his army to the River Boyne, near Drogheda, just north of Dublin. On 1st July 1690 a pitched battle was fought, but William's superior forces quickly overran James's army, though William graciously allowed James to escape into exile, thus ending his attempt to reclaim the throne.

▱ BILL OF RIGHTS

Early in 1689 Parliament drew up the Declaration of Rights (William and Mary are shown accepting the Bill), which was afterwards consolidated as the Bill of Rights. It is usually seen as the second most important piece of constitutional legislation after the Magna Carta and reduced royal power considerably. Its most important clauses were that no Catholic could ever become the ruling monarch and taxes and laws could be implemented only with parliamentary consent.

1690	freedom of religion in Ireland.	**1694**	the Electress Sophia of Hanover.	**1701**
James defeated again at Battle of the Boyne by William's forces.	**1692** Glencoe Massacre ordered by William.	Mary II dies; William rules alone.	**1701** William agrees a grand alliance between England, Holland and Austria.	War of Spanish Succession breaks out.
1691 Treaty of Limerick allows	**1694** The Bank of England founded.	**1701** Act of Settlement settles the line of succession on		**1702** William III dies in a hunting accident.

🗋 GOVERNMENT   ⚗ HEALTH & MEDICINE   ⚖ JUSTICE   ✝ RELIGION   📄 SCIENCE

ANNE

BORN 1665 • ACCEDED 1702 • DIED 1714

AGE OF ELEGANCE

Anne's name was given to a period of simple, yet elegant furniture and interior decoration design, though she had nothing to do with it. Although attractive in her youth, in later years Anne herself was anything but elegant. She was grossly overweight and suffered from numerous ailments, including obesity and gout, having to be carried about in a chair. She had 18 pregnancies but all of her children died in childbirth or infancy, which probably contributed to her general ill-health.

RACING AT ASCOT

Anne introduced horse racing at Ascot in 1711, thus beginning a long royal patronage that still exists today.

A nne was the second daughter of James II and Anne Hyde. She succeeded William III, her brother-in-law, in 1702, when he died without leaving an heir. She was the last Stuart monarch to rule this country. Her short reign was a strong one, bolstered by a series of military victories on the continent, which established Britain as the most powerful country in Europe. During this period also, Parliament consolidated its constitutional successes, making the British government one of the strongest and most democratic institutions then known, and the envy of other European countries.

BLENHEIM PALACE

Blenheim Palace was commissioned by Queen Anne, paid for partly by national funds, and given as a reward to John Churchill, Duke of Marlborough, in recognition of his great victories in the war with France. It was designed by John Vanbrugh and begun in 1705, though it was still incomplete when Churchill died in 1722. It now ranks as one of the most magnificent stately homes in Europe.

FIRST NEWSPAPER

Although various newsletters had been in circulation for some time, the first proper daily newspaper in London, the 'Daily Courant', was published in 1702, giving the general population access to news and events, as they happened, for the first time.

MONARCHY'S LAST VETO

Anne was the last monarch to veto a parliamentary bill, in 1708, when she objected to a new law to reorganise the Scottish militia. The monarchy still reserves the right of veto today, but in practice all bills receive royal approval as a matter of course.

1702
Anne, William's Sister-in-law and James II's second daughter, succeeds to the throne.

1702
First daily newspaper in London, the Daily Courant, published.
1704
England and her allies,

under Marlborough, defeat French at Battle of Blenheim.
1704
Gibraltar taken from Spain.
1705
Barcelona captured

from Spanish.
1706
French defeated at Battle of Ramilles.
1707
Act of Union unites

the parliaments of England and Scotland.
1707
Henry Fielding, claimed to be founder of the novel form of writing, was born.

🏛 ARCHITECTURE   📖 ARTS & LITERATURE   🏳 EXPLORATION   🔦 FAMOUS BATTLES

📜 ACT OF UNION

When James VI of Scotland was crowned as James I of England, the crowns of those two countries were united, but Scotland retained its own parliament. In 1707, however, the Act of Union was passed, uniting the governments of the two countries. The Scottish parliament was abolished, Scotland instead sending 45 members and 16 peers to the new Parliament of Great Britain in London.

💣 BATTLE OF BLENHEIM

Britain emerged from the War of the Spanish Succession as the greatest power in Europe, having won several notable victories under the leadership of John Churchill, Duke of Marlborough. The greatest of these was the Battle of Blenheim, fought in 1704 between the allies and the French at Blenheim, in Bavaria. The French were routed, suffering heavy losses with an estimated 26,000 dead and 15,000 captured. The War finally ended in April 1713.

📜 ACT OF SETTLEMENT

In 1701 the Act of Settlement was passed which ensured that the line of succession should pass to the Electress Sophia of Hanover, or her heirs, who were Protestants and distantly related to the Stuarts. In the event, Anne died childless and so the crown passed to James I's great-grandson, who became George I, rather than to Anne's Catholic half-brother James, the 'Old Pretender'.

📜 LAST EXECUTION FOR WITCHCRAFT

Witchcraft was still punishable by death and in 1712 the last execution of a witch took place. Practising witchcraft remained a punishable offence up until 1736 when it was abolished as a crime, in recognition that most so-called witches were not practising pagan rites but were merely local wise-women, or healers practising herbal medicine.

DUKE OF MARLBOROUGH

John Churchill was born in 1650 to a Devonshire family of quite humble status. At the age of 17 he took up military service and quickly rose to a position of distinction in the Dutch wars. At first he fought alongside James II but later changed his allegiance to William III. However, it was during the War of the Spanish Succession, between France and the allied armies of England, Holland and Austria that Churchill really came into his own, winning a series of magnificent victories that turned the tide of the war against France. He was created Duke of Marlborough in 1702.

1709
Gabriel Fahrenheit makes first alcohol thermometer.
1711
Duke of Marlborough falls into disrepute and

is dismissed from commanding the army.
1711
Queen establishes royal patronage of horse racing at Ascot.

1712
Last execution for witchcraft in England, though it is still a crime.
1712
Jonathan Swift

proposes an English Academy to 'fix' the English language.
1713
End of War of Spanish Succession.

1714
Sophia of Hanover dies, making her son George heir to the English throne.
1714
Queen Anne dies.

📜 GOVERNMENT   ⚕ HEALTH & MEDICINE   ⚖ JUSTICE   ✝ RELIGION   🧪 SCIENCE

GEORGE I

BORN 1660 • ACCEDED 1714 • DIED 1727

George I was the first Hanoverian monarch of Britain, marking a period of great change in the constitution. In 1701 the Act of Settlement had been passed, which ensured that a Catholic monarch could never again sit on the British throne. When Anne died in 1714 without leaving an heir, she was the last Stuart monarch and succession passed to George of Hanover, great-grandson of James I and Anne's distant cousin, her closest relative. George had little interest in Britain and could speak no English, so it became necessary for many of his governmental duties to be transferred to Parliament and his ministers.

SIR ROBERT WALPOLE (1676-1745)

A member of the Whig (Liberal) party, Sir Robert Walpole dominated British political life, particularly during the period 1721-42. As George became more and more reliant on his politicians to govern the country, Walpole took the opportunity of increasing the power and influence of the House of Commons. In 1721 he became the First Lord of the Treasury, the most powerful position in Parliament, and became, in effect, the first Prime Minister.

JACOBITE REBELLION (1715)

George's accession to the British throne was not a popular choice, especially in Scotland, where a rebellion broke out to place a Stuart back on the throne. The rebellion was led by James Edward Stuart, son of the deposed James II, known as the 'Old Pretender'. The rising did not progress beyond Scotland and was soon put down.

SOUTH SEA BUBBLE

In 1711 a speculative company was set up to trade with South America, under a treaty with Spain. The Government invested heavily and encouraged many others to do likewise. Many thousands, in the hope of becoming rich, invested their savings in the company, which became grossly over-subscribed. When the 'bubble burst' in 1720, many faced financial ruin.

1714	Townsend and Robert	Stuart, the 'Old Pretender'	**1717**	**1718**
George I succeeds his	Walpole as leaders.	on the throne.	Sir Robert Walpole	Quadruple Alliance
cousin Anne to the throne.	**1715**	**1716**	resigns from	between Britain,
1714	Jacobite rebellion in	The Septennial Act calls	government following	France, Austria
New Whig government	Scotland fails in its	for General Elections	Townsend's dismissal	and Netherlands
elected with Charles	attempt to put James	every seven years.	from the government.	against Spain.

🏛 ARCHITECTURE   📖 ARTS & LITERATURE   🖋 EXPLORATION   💣 FAMOUS BATTLES

WILLIAM HOGARTH (1697-1764)

William Hogarth became the most important English artist
of his time, turning away from foreign influences and
establishing a style of his own. He painted a series of pictures
which told a sequence of contemporary moral tales,
establishing him as both an artist and a satirist. He went on
to produce a series of sharply witty and satirical engravings
which are important for the subject matter they portray,
like the hypocrisy of religion, the horror of asylums (above)
and the appalling social conditions of the day.

SOPHIA DOROTHEA

George married Sophia Dorothea, the beautiful but
arrogant daughter of his countryman, the Duke of Celle,
in 1682, before he became King of England. It was a
loveless marriage and after she bore him two children
they went their separate ways. George had several
illicit liaisons, while Sophia had an affair with Count
Philip von Konigsmarck, of Sweden. Despite having
mistresses of his own, George was infuriated. He had
the Count killed and banished his wife from court.

📖 SAMUEL JOHNSON
(1709–84)

*A writer, critic and lexicographer
(someone who studies words), Samuel
Johnson is famous for compiling the
first proper 'Dictionary of the English
Language'. First published in 1755,
it took him 9 years to compile and
contained over 40,000 entries.*

📜 SEPTENNIAL ACT

*In 1716 The Septennial Act was passed
in Parliament which decreed that
General Elections should be held every
seven years. This level of freedom to
vote for one's government was unheard
of in George's native Germany, and
most of Europe, at the time.*

📖 DANIEL DEFOE
(1660–1731)

*Daniel Defoe started his writing career
as a pamphleteer (what we today would
term a journalist) and was imprisoned
for his outspoken views. It was during a
spell in prison that he wrote 'Robinson
Crusoe' (below), which was published in
1719 and is generally regarded by most
as the first truly great English novel.*

1719
'Robinson Crusoe' published
by Daniel Defoe; generally
regarded as first 'great' novel.
1720
South Sea Bubble, a
speculative company,
bursts, causing widespread
financial ruin.
1721
Sir Robert Walpole
reinstated and becomes
first Prime Minister as
First Lord of the Treasury.
1722
Duke of Marlborough dies.
1725
Treaty of Hanover,
forms an alliance
between Britain, France,
Prussia and other northern
European countries.
1726
Edinburgh opens
first circulating library.
1727
Sir Isaac
Newton dies.
1727
George I dies.

📗 GOVERNMENT   ⚗ HEALTH & MEDICINE   ⚖ JUSTICE   ✝ RELIGION   📜 SCIENCE

GEORGE II

BORN 1683 • ACCEDED 1727 • DIED 1760

*U*nder the expert guidance of Sir Robert Walpole the first third of George's reign was one of peace and great prosperity. The Prime Minister skilfully steered Britain away from all wars in Europe, but after he retired from politics, the remainder of George's reign was spent in one conflict or another, including war with Spain and two separate conflicts with France. During his reign also, the British Empire acquired considerable new domains.

JAMES WOLFE

James Wolfe, although of a frail constitution, proved a courageous and extremely capable commander. He joined the army as a boy and by the age of 16 had already become an officer. He quickly rose through the ranks to become a captain at 17, lieutenant-colonel at 23 and major general soon after. He was actively involved in the 'Seven Years' War' with France and led the attack on Quebec in 1759, which secured Canada as part of the British Empire, though he was killed in the process.

WILLIAM PITT THE ELDER (1708–78)

Of humble birth, William Pitt was known as the 'Great Commoner'. He was a politician of rare genius, though he suffered from ill-health, including bouts of mental illness, which may have impaired his judgement on occasion. He became Prime Minister of a coalition government in 1757 and again, as a Whig, between 1766-67. As Secretary of State he led Britain to victory against France in the 'Seven Years' War', establishing Britain as the most powerful world power.

CAROLINE OF BRANDENBURG-ANSBACH

George married Caroline in 1705 and together they had 10 children. She remained faithful to him, even though he had numerous affairs. He never remarried after her death in 1737. She was plump, but not unattractive, and possessed great charm and intelligence, striking up a life-long, though strictly professional, friendship with Sir Robert Walpole.

1727
George II succeeds his father to the throne.

1732
Royal Charter issued to found Georgia in America.

1736
Witchcraft abolished as a crime.

1738
Wesley brothers found the Methodist movement.

1739
War of Captain Jenkins' Ear breaks out with Spain.

1740
War of Austrian Succession breaks out.

1742
Sir Robert Walpole resigns as Prime Minster.

1743
George leads his army into battle at

Dettingen, Bavaria, one of the last occasions when ruling monarch led troops in war.

1745
Sir Robert Walpole dies.

🏛 ARCHITECTURE   📖 ARTS & LITERATURE   ✒ EXPLORATION   💣 FAMOUS BATTLES

JACOBITE REBELLION (1745)

The second Jacobite rebellion, although ending in failure, was a much more serious attempt to place the Catholic Stuarts back on the throne. The word Jacobite comes from the Latin word for James, 'Jacobus', and is the name adopted by the supporters of James II and his heirs. This second rising was led by Charles Edward Stuart (the 'Young Pretender') known as 'Bonnie Prince Charlie'. He achieved early success against the English at the Battle of Prestonpans in July 1745 but by the following April he was defeated. He escaped to exile in France (aided by Flora Macdonald) and died penniless in 1788.

WITCHCRAFT

In country areas, many of the old ways, such as herbal remedies, were still practised and many villages supported a local 'wise-woman'. Such things were little understood by the church and the authorities, who saw it as witchcraft. Until 1712 the practising of witchcraft was still punishable by death and it remained a crime right up until 1736.

WAR OF CAPTAIN JENKINS'S EAR

In 1739 Britain declared war with its old enemy, Spain. The incident that is said to have sparked off the conflict took place during a skirmish in the South Seas. Spain had long been subjected to piratical raids by the English and during one such raid an English captain named Jenkins had his ear cut off. Whether or not the story is true is debatable, but open hostilities did break out between the two countries.

BRITISH MUSEUM

As an outward show of Britain's growing Empire and world power, a new, national museum was founded in London in 1753, known as the British Museum. It opened six years later and was partly paid for out of proceeds from a lottery. In addition to displaying artefacts gathered from the colonies, the museum quickly became regarded as one of the finest such educational institutions in the world.

📖 HANDEL (1685–1759)

George Frederick Handel, musician and composer, came to live in England in 1712 and soon became a favourite at court. His great love was for choral works, several based on Biblical stories, such as 'The Messiah', first performed in 1742, and 'Music for Royal Fireworks', performed in 1748 to celebrate the end of the war of the Austrian Succession.

✝ JOHN WESLEY (1703–91)

John Wesley, together with his brother Charles, founded a new, non-conformist Protestant church known as the Methodists, so called because of their strict religious observance. The order was formed by Charles in 1738, but it was when John Wesley joined the movement soon afterwards that it really caught the popular imagination. Wesley was a fine orator and frequently gave open-air sermons that attracted huge audiences of 20,000 or more.

💣 BATTLE OF CULLODEN

The hopes and dreams of the Jacobite rebels came to an end at the Battle of Culloden in April 1746. The English, under the Duke of Cumberland, inflicted a massive defeat on the Scots, thus ending the Stuart claim to the throne once and for all. For many years after, even the wearing of kilts and the playing of bagpipes was punishable by death.

↗ CLIVE OF INDIA (1725–74)

At the same time as Wolfe was winning victories against the French in North America, Robert Clive was doing likewise in India. In 1757 he won the Battle of Plessey, thus adding India to the Empire, and was appointed governor of Bengal. However, he was hated by the Indians and was censured for misgovernment; he later committed suicide in London.

1745 *Second Jacobite rebellion meets with Scottish victory at Prestonpans.* **1746** *Jacobites beaten at*	*Battle of Culloden.* **1751** *George's eldest son, Frederick, dies. His son, George becomes heir.*	**1753** *British Museum founded in London.* **1756/63** *Seven Years' War with France.*	**1757** *Robert Clive acquires Indian province of Bengal for Britain.* **1757** *William Pitt, the Elder, becomes Prime Minister.*	**1759** *Wolfe captures Quebec from French, secures Canada as English colony.* **1760** *George II dies.*

🛒 **GOVERNMENT**   🥄 **HEALTH & MEDICINE**   ⚖️ **JUSTICE**   ✝ **RELIGION**   🧪 **SCIENCE**

📖 JANE AUSTEN

Jane Austen (1775-1817) was a clergyman's daughter from Hampshire who liked to write stories as a young girl to amuse herself. Several of these, including 'Pride and Prejudice', were later reworked as socially witty novels. She wrote from personal experience only so her work gives us valuable insights into the snobbery and morality of Georgian society.

📜 ACT OF UNION WITH IRELAND

During the 17th and 18th centuries many Protestants had been encouraged to settle in Ireland to help keep the country loyal to England. In 1798 a rebellion to unite Catholics and Protestants against England failed. In response, the Act of Union was passed in 1800, making Ireland part of the U.K.

🏴 AUSTRALIA DISCOVERED

Although Dutch sailors had discovered Australia some time before, it was the voyages of Captain Cook between 1768–79 that opened up the country for colonisation. Many new plants and animals were discovered, including the kangaroo.

THE FRENCH REVOLUTION

The growing tide of social unrest in Europe resulted, in 1798, in open revolution in France, leading to the eventual overthrow of the monarchy and the execution of Louis XVI.

A DEVOTED QUEEN

On 8th September 1761 George married Charlotte of Mecklenburg-Strelitz. Tradition has it that it was an arranged marriage and they met for the first time only on the afternoon of the wedding. The early years of their marriage were very happy and they had 15 children. Charlotte was intelligent and vivacious in her youth, but became quite obese in later life. She grew to love George and remained devoted to him throughout his earlier bouts of illness, but gradually grew away from him in later life. Sadly, the king did not recognise her when she died in 1818 aged 75.

KEW PALACE

In 1730, Kew House and gardens were acquired by George III. His mother, Princess Augusta, began a nine acre botanical garden and study centre there in 1759.

A PRIME MINISTER ASSASSINATED

On 12th May 1812 Spencer Perceval, the Prime Minister, was assassinated in the lobby of the House of Commons by an insane bankrupt, Francis Bellingham.

1760 George III succeeds his grandfather as king.	**1763** Seven Years War ends with 'Peace of Paris'.	colonies and leads eventually to War of American Independence.	around the world. **1773** Boston Tea Party.	**1783** America recognised by Britain as a nation in own right.
1760 Start of the Industrial Revolution in Britain.	**1765** Stamp Act raises taxes in American	**1769/70** James Cook's first epic voyage of discovery	**1775/83** American War of Independence.	**1783** William Pitt, the Younger,

🏛 ARCHITECTURE   📖 ARTS & LITERATURE   🏴 EXPLORATION   🛢 FAMOUS BATTLES

GEORGE III

BORN 1738 • ACCEDED 1760 • DIED 1820

George III was the first of the Hanoverian monarchs to be born in England. He succeeded to the throne in 1760 on the death of his grandfather, George II, and took an immediate interest in affairs of state. Unlike his two predecessors, he regarded himself as English and the people warmed to his simple, direct manner. He was plagued by ill health in later years and in 1811 his son was created Prince Regent. His long reign spanned almost the entire period now termed the 'Industrial Revolution' and saw many changes, but he is perhaps best remembered for the loss of the American colonies in 1783.

FARMER GEORGE

George always regarded himself as an ordinary man. He was very hard-working and took a strong interest in government. From an early age he also showed a keen interest in farming and liked to chat to workers on the royal farms, earning him the nickname 'Farmer George'.

THE NAPOLEONIC WARS

Within a few years of the French Revolution, France began to assert itself as a major power in Europe, under the leadership of Napoleon Bonaparte. War broke out between Britain and France in 1793 and resumed again in 1803, after a short truce. Napoleon was finally defeated at the Battle of Waterloo in 1815.

MENTAL ILLNESS

From 1788 George suffered periods of mental instability and was kept locked away. Modern research, however, would suggest that he was not mad but suffering from a disease called porphyria.

becomes Prime Minister.	**1800**	**1805**	spell of illness.	at Battle
1789	Act of Union passed between	Nelson defeats French at	**1812**	of Waterloo.
Outbreak of French Revolution.	Britain and Ireland.	Battle of Trafalgar.	Spencer Perceval, Prime	**1815**
1793	**1803/15**	**1811**	Minister, assassinated.	Corn Laws passed.
War breaks out between	Napoleonic Wars between	George III's son become	**1815**	**1820**
Britain and France again.	England and France.	Regent during prolonged	Napoleon defeated	George III dies.

GOVERNMENT   HEALTH & MEDICINE   JUSTICE   RELIGION   SCIENCE

LOSS OF THE AMERICAN COLONIES

(1775–1783)

The American War of Independence was the first colonial revolt in the British Empire. The government at home completely misread the situation, scarcely believing that such a revolt was possible. The revolt could perhaps have been avoided if they had listened to the grievances of the colonists, especially with regard to taxes, and when the French supported them against the English, the conclusion was inevitable. Although the war did not finally end until 1783, after eight years of bitter struggle, the outcome was effectively decided after the British surrender of Yorktown two years previously in 1781.

GEORGE WASHINGTON
(1732–99)

George Washington was born in Virginia and traced his ancestry back to a Northamptonshire farming family. He fought for the English in the French and Indian wars of 1754–63. In 1775 he was made commander-in-chief of Continental forces and led the revolution against England. He became the first President of the newly founded United States of America and served two terms between 1787–97. He refused a third term and retired to his home at Mount Vernon, Virginia.

GEORGE III

George III was the last British monarch to preside over the American colonies. His Prime Minister, Lord North, proved incapable of handling the situation properly and is held to be largely responsible for the loss of the colonies by misreading the seriousness of the revolt.

ALLIANCE WITH FRANCE

In 1777, following the British defeat at Saratoga, the French recognised the American states as an independent nation and sent military aid. The British and French had long been engaged in war across the globe, fiercely contesting colonial rule and the American war presented a golden opportunity for France to deliver a crushing blow to her old adversary.

ARCHITECTURE   ARTS & LITERATURE   EXPLORATION   FAMOUS BATTLES

BOSTON TEA PARTY

The action that prompted the start of the War of Independence began in 1765 with the Stamp Act, which increased taxes dramatically in the American colonies. It was followed five years later by the Boston Massacre, when British troops opened fire on a group of rebelling, but unarmed civilians, killing five. The situation rapidly worsened and in December 1773 a group of colonists disguised themselves as Indians and emptied the contents of over 300 tea chests into Boston harbour in protest at the high taxes imposed by the British government. Open conflict began in 1775.

SARATOGA

The early engagements of the war went well for the British and for a while it looked as though the revolt would be easily put down. The tide of the war turned in 1777, however, when General Howe suffered a humiliating defeat at the hands of the colonists, under Washington, at the Battle of Saratoga.

YORKTOWN

The Battle of Yorktown, Virginia, fought on 19th October 1781, marked the real end of the war. The British, led by General Cornwallis, became cut off by a combined American and French force greatly superior in numbers. The humiliated Cornwallis was forced to surrender. It was the last major battle of the war and although the British fought on in a number of minor skirmishes, the position was hopeless and the outcome of the war had already been decided. The British are shown (left) surrendering to General Washington in 1781. Britain recognised the independence of the American colonies.

DECLARATION OF INDEPENDENCE

In protest at the British government's implementation of high taxes from far-off London, the colonists revolted claiming that there should be 'no taxation without representation'. The Declaration of Independence was issued on 4th July 1776 following a delegation, headed by Thomas Jefferson and Benjamin Franklin, at the Continental Congress.

GOVERNMENT   HEALTH & MEDICINE   JUSTICE   RELIGION   SCIENCE

CATO STREET CONSPIRACY

In 1820, in the wake of the French Revolution, a plot was hatched by a group of conspirators, led by Arthur Thistlewood, to assassinate the entire British cabinet. Thistlewood was to be proclaimed president of a new-style of government, but the plotters were betrayed and they were arrested at their headquarters in Cato Street, London.

NATIONAL GALLERY

George was a great patron of the arts, commissioning many paintings and works of architecture. He established the National Gallery in London in 1824 in which to house a national collection of art, accessible to all.

MRS. FITZHERBERT

The Act of Settlement, passed in 1701, forbade George (heir to the throne) to marry a Catholic, but he married his Catholic mistress, Maria Fitzherbert, in secret in 1785. The marriage was never officially recognised and the Reverend Robert Burt, who performed the ceremony in London, was later transferred to the remote marshland parish of St.Mary Hoo, near Rochester in Kent, to live out his life in obscurity.

FIRST PUBLIC RAILWAY

Thomas Newcomen developed the first practical steam engine about 1712 and the first successful steam-powered locomotives were built in 1808 by Richard Trevithick, a Cornish mining engineer. The first railway to use steam from the start was the Stockton-Darlington Railway, which opened in 1825 followed, in 1833, by the world's first public railway.

TURNPIKE ROADS

In the Georgian period Britain's roads had fallen into a shocking state of disrepair. A series of laws was passed which allowed for Turnpike Trusts to be formed. Their purpose was to build new roads with stone and tarmacadam surfaces, paid for by charging a toll to all those who used them. They were hated by the poor and the drovers, who could not afford the tolls, but by 1830 there were over 20,500 miles (33,000 kilometres) of turnpike roads in Britain.

ROBERT PEEL

The first organised civilian police force was introduced in London in 1829 by Sir Robert Peel, later Prime Minister. There had been various attempts at patrolling the streets against crime since the Middle Ages, but the 'Peelers', as they came to be known, were the first force to be properly recruited and paid for from public funds. Many of those recruited were ex-servicemen, home from the wars, and the force was run along military lines.

ARCHITECTURE   ARTS & LITERATURE   EXPLORATION   FAMOUS BATTLES

GEORGE IV

BORN 1762 • ACCEDED 1820 • DIED 1830

aving spent the better part of his life in his father's shadow, George IV's reign was a comparatively short one. Always prone to excesses, particularly during his Regency, he changed from a handsome, popular prince into a debauched and obese caricature of his former self. As part of a deal to get Parliament to pay off his mounting debts, George had to marry his cousin, Caroline of Brunswick, in 1795. It was a loveless match and George refused to allow her to be present at his Coronation.

THE REGENCY

George's father, George III, suffered frequent bouts of what was then thought to be madness, but is now generally recognised as porphyria. During these periods, the ageing king was considered unfit to govern. In 1811 his son became Regent, as Prince George, taking over many of the constitutional roles of his father.

BRIGHTON PAVILION

Whilst still Prince Regent, George commissioned John Nash to redesign his seaside home at Brighton (where he stayed when taking his regular sea-water health cures) and convert it into a palace. Nash used his skill and ingenuity to unify the Prince's fascination with oriental and Indian art into the extravaganza of Brighton Pavilion, which still survives intact.

1824
National Gallery founded in London.
1825
World's first public railway system is opened between

Stockton and Darlington.
1828
The Duke of Wellington becomes Prime Minister.
1829
Sir Robert Peel

sets up the world's first organised police force.
1829
First horse-drawn buses appear

in London.
1829
Catholic Relief Act passed, allowing Catholics to become M.P.s.

1830
George Stephenson's 'Rocket' wins 'Rainhill Trials' in Liverpool.
1830
George IV dies.

GOVERNMENT   HEALTH & MEDICINE   JUSTICE   RELIGION   SCIENCE

WILLIAM IV

BORN 1765 • ACCEDED 1830 • DIED 1837

A s the third son of George III, William could never have expected to become king and only did so, at the age of 64, on the death of his brother, George. His short reign was one of great constitutional change and political reform. He had 10 illegitimate children by his mistress, Dorothea Jordan. He later married Princess Adelaide of Saxe-Meiningen, but they had no children.

'SILLY BILLY'

William joined the navy at 13 and quickly rose to the rank of captain. He had a forthright manner and was prone to making tactless remarks, which earned him the nickname 'Silly Billy', particularly with regard to his sometimes inept but nevertheless enthusiastic attempts at government. To be fair, however, he was likeable and lacked his brother's extravagances, which endeared him to the people.

FACTORY ACT

Until the Factory Act was passed in 1833 (which reduced the working week to 60 hours and prohibited children under the age of 9 from working) conditions in the factories were appalling. Until then, children as young as five could be set to work and the average working day was 14 hours, including Saturdays.

SLAVERY ABOLISHED

After years of campaigning by such people as William Wilberforce, slavery was finally abolished throughout the Empire in 1833. The law met with a great deal of opposition, particularly in the colonies, where rich landowners relied heavily on slave labour. Slaves were captured from the poorer regions of the world, such as Africa, and transported to the colonies, where they became the property of rich landowners. A slave purchased for as little as £3 in Africa might fetch £24 at auction in America.

DOROTHEA JORDAN

William lived with his mistress Dorothea Jordan, an actress, almost as man and wife for 21 years. She bore him 10 illegitimate children. Financial pressures forced him to marry Adelaide of Saxe-Meiningen in 1818. Whether he continued his affair with Dorothea is not known.

🏛 ARCHITECTURE   📖 ARTS & LITERATURE   🖋 EXPLORATION   ⚫ FAMOUS BATTLES

TOLPUDDLE MARTYRS

In 1834, six villagers from Tolpuddle, in Dorset, were arrested for joining a trade union, which at that time was still illegal. A march was organised by many who supported the six and a petition presented to the king, but to no avail. The villagers were tried and sentenced to seven years' hard labour in Australia, although they were afterwards allowed to return.

POOR LAW

In 1834 the Poor Law was passed which took the responsibility of caring for the poor away from the parishes in which they lived. The new law provided workhouses in which the poor and homeless could receive food and lodging in return for giving a day's labour. Conditions were harsh and the rewards low, but it did succeed in reducing the number of homeless beggars who slept rough on the street. Many of the poor, who had lost their jobs on the land, were forced to seek work in the crowded and dirty industrial towns.

PARLIAMENT BURNS DOWN

Parliament formerly met in part of the old royal palace of Westminster given to the Commons by Edward VI. The building burned down in a disastrous fire in 1834. The present Houses of Parliament were completed in 1867 to designs by Pugin and Barry.

📜 FIRST REFORM ACT

William's reign saw a number of important legal and political reforms including, in 1832, the First Reform Act, which attempted to reform the voting system. The vote was extended to property owners, land owners and some tenants, and a fairer, more proportional system of allocating parliamentary seats was introduced.

📜 MUNICIPAL REFORM ACT

The Municipal Reform Act, passed in 1835, brought political reforms to local government. It required the members of town councils to be elected by ratepayers and not by the businessmen of a town. It also made councils accountable by ordering them to publish details of their financial dealings.

📜 REGISTRATION ACT

With the burgeoning population caused by the Industrial Revolution and the massive population movements it caused from country to town, it was decided that a greater check was needed on the people of Britain. In 1836 the registration of all births, marriages and deaths became compulsory by law.

workhouses for the poor.
1834
Tolpuddle Martyrs transported to Australia for their efforts to form a trade union

which was illegal.
1834
Palace of Westminster (Houses of Parliament) virtually destroyed by fire.

1835
Screw propeller invented, independently, in both Britain and America.
1835
Municipal Reform Act

passed making it compulsory to elect town councils and publish accounts of public records.
1836
Registration of births,

marriages and deaths made compulsory.
1837
Colour printing invented.
1837
William IV dies.

📜 GOVERNMENT   ⚕ HEALTH & MEDICINE   ⚖ JUSTICE   ✝ RELIGION   🏛 SCIENCE

📖 CHARLES DICKENS (1812-70)

Charles Dickens was the greatest and most popular novelist of his day and even today his works are seldom out of print. He became a spokesman for his time with his graphic descriptions of Victorian England. All of his books were serialised, making them available to all classes. He spent the last years of his life at Gad's Hill Place, Higham, in Kent, and died there while working on his last, unfinished novel, 'The Mystery of Edwin Drood'.

📜 PEOPLE'S CHARTER

Soon into Victoria's reign, the People's Charter was issued in 1838 by a group of political reformers known as the Chartists. Its main clauses called for the right to vote for everyone, the right for anyone to seek election, secret ballots and equal representation, among others. Although not fully realised until 1944, it forms the basis of our modern parliamentary system.

🥣 SMALLPOX VACCINATION

A number of deadly diseases were prevalent in Victorian Britain, one of the worst and most contagious of which was smallpox. Several doctors, including Edward Jenner, carried out pioneering work in developing vaccines to control the spread of such diseases, though many people were afraid to take them. So, in 1853, a law was passed which made vaccination against smallpox compulsory, as part of the government's policy of health and social reforms.

BOER WAR

Between 1899 -1902 a war was fought between Britain and a group of Dutch settlers in South Africa, known as the Boers. A massive army was sent against the Boers, but it proved largely ineffective against the settlers' guerrilla tactics. Peace was eventually reached in 1902, after much loss of life on both sides.

PRINCE ALBERT

Victoria married Prince Albert of Saxe-Coburg-Gotha in 1840 and together they had nine children. It was truly a love match and they were a devoted couple. Albert was intelligent and talented and proved to be an able administrator. He designed the royal houses of Osborne (on the Isle of Wight) and Balmoral (in the Scottish Highlands) and also instigated the Great Exhibition, believing that by promoting industry it would generate more work and so help the poor. Proceeds from the profits were used to fund various public institutes, including many of London's museums. When he died, prematurely, in 1861 at the age of 42 from typhoid, the queen went into mourning for 13 years and had a number of buildings and monuments, including the Albert Hall, erected in his honour.

1837	1840	1841	1846	1852
Victoria succeeds her uncle to the throne.	*Victoria marries Albert of Saxe-Coburg-Gotha.*	*Sir Robert Peel becomes Prime Minister.*	*Corn Laws repealed.*	*Duke of Wellington dies.*
1838	**1840**	**1845/48**	**1851**	**1854/56**
People's Charter issued for political reform.	*Penny postal service introduced.*	*Potato Famine in Ireland.*	*Great Exhibition in London initiated by Prince Albert.*	*Crimean War between Britain (and France) against Russia.*

🏛 ARCHITECTURE　　📖 ARTS & LITERATURE　　🖋 EXPLORATION　　⬥ FAMOUS BATTLES

VICTORIA

BORN 1819 • ACCEDED 1837 • DIED 1901

ictoria came to the throne at the age of 18 after her uncle, William IV, died childless in 1837. She was destined to become our longest reigning monarch and ruler of the greatest empire the world has ever seen. She came to the throne with enthusiasm and consulted frequently with her ministers. Some of our greatest prime ministers came to power during her long reign, including Lord Melbourne, Sir Robert Peel, Gladstone and Disraeli.

GREAT EXHIBITION

The Great Exhibition of 1851 was the brainchild of Prince Albert. Britain was known as the 'workshop of the world' and the exhibition was intended as a shop window, an outward display of the country's achievements. It was a runaway success and attracted over six million visitors. It was held in the purpose-built Crystal Palace, a masterpiece of glass and cast iron, designed by Joseph Paxton. The building covered over 26 acres and was moved from its site in Hyde Park to Sydenham after the exhibition, but sadly burned down in 1936.

PENNY POST SERVICE

Although private postal services had been in operation since at least Tudor times, no national postal system existed until 1840 when the Penny Post was introduced. This revolutionised the delivery of letters when, for the small payment of 1d. (0.4p) a letter could be sent anywhere in the country. The first stamp issued was the Penny Black and the very next day John Tomlinson became the world's first stamp collector.

IRISH POTATO FAMINE

Many of the people of Ireland lived at subsistence level, surviving on a meagre diet, mostly consisting of potatoes. When a serious blight hit the potato crop in 1845 many died of starvation. Between 1845-49 about 1.3 million people died, while about the same number emigrated in an effort to find a better life.

CRIMEAN WAR

The Crimean War was fought between Britain and Russia (1854-56) on a peninsula that is now part of modern-day Turkey. The 'Charge of the Light Brigade' took place during this war at the Battle of Balaclava in 1854. It was one of Britain's worst military disasters, resulting in the deaths or serious wounding of nearly half of the cavalrymen of the Light Brigade. Casualties in the war were high with many of the injured being cared for by Florence Nightingale and her team of nurses.

1856 Victoria Cross first introduced for bravery in wartime. **1857** Indian Mutiny against	British rule. **1867** Canada declared first country within the British Empire to become an independent dominion.	**1869** Irish Church is disestablished. **1870** Education becomes compulsory for all children.	**1872** Secret voting introduced at elections. **1876** Victoria becomes Empress of India.	**1889/1902** Boer War breaks out in South Africa. **1901** Victoria dies; our longest reigning monarch.

GOVERNMENT   HEALTH & MEDICINE   JUSTICE   RELIGION   SCIENCE

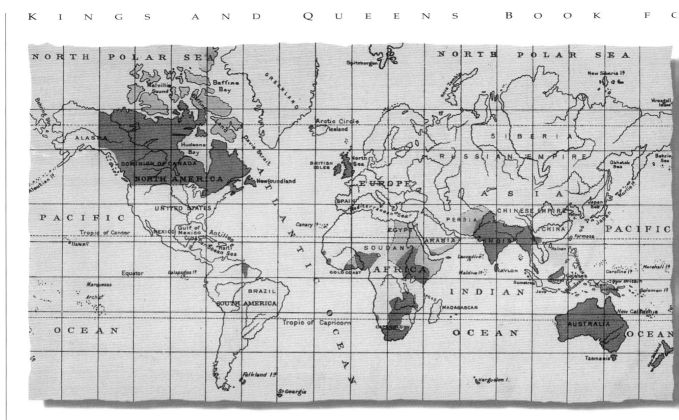

EXTENT OF THE EMPIRE

This map shows the full extent of the Empire. All of the countries under British control are coloured orange. They included such distant lands as Canada, Australia, New Zealand, India, parts of Indonesia and the Far East, large tracts of Africa and several islands in the southern oceans, used as convenient outposts and trading posts for the merchant fleets of the Empire. As a direct result of the Empire, the English language is now the most widespread and commonly spoken language in the world.

LARGEST EMPIRE EVER KNOWN

Because it was not conceived as a single plan, the British Empire grew very slowly, allowing new colonies to be consolidated and gradually brought under British control. At its beginnings in the 16th century it consisted only of a handful of settlements in North America and grew hardly at all during the 17th century. Under the Georges, the boundaries were stretched further, coming to the full height of its power under Victoria. At its greatest extent the Empire covered one quarter of the land mass of the world; the largest empire ever known.

THE COMMONWEALTH

In many respects, a large part of the British Empire still exists, known today as the Commonwealth. Although few countries take kindly to being governed by strangers, and Britain ruthlessly exploited the riches of countries under its control, many prospered under British rule. The British way of life was spread round the world and many of the advantages of modern civilisation were shared with less well-off countries. Initially, attempts at independence were stoutly resisted, but gradually all of the Empire's member states received their independence, most without resorting to violence, and most countries retain friendly relations with Britain, earning a respect no other empire can claim.

🏛 ARCHITECTURE   📖 ARTS & LITERATURE   ↬ EXPLORATION   ⬥ FAMOUS BATTLES

THE BRITISH EMPIRE

The expansion of the British Empire had more to do with trade and the wealth it generated than with world domination as a super power, which is possibly why it was so successful. Although obviously aided by the military, it was not itself militarily-led. Unlike other great empires, such as the Romans, who conquered other lands, the British Empire concentrated more on controlling the economy and ultimately the government of other countries. Also, unlike other empires, its dominions were acquired in a piecemeal fashion at different times, stretching in an ad hoc fashion across the globe, instead of following a coherent pattern radiating out from its imperial centre.

VICTORIA-EMPRESS OF INDIA

While many of the lands taken over by Britain were relatively unsophisticated before our arrival, India was, by contrast, a land of great antiquity, with a rich cultural history. Britain's original settlements there were minimal and controlled by a commercial company, the East India Company, with protection by the British army. Following a mutiny in 1857-58, however, Britain assumed full control of India. Queen Victoria was created Empress of India, and all subsequent kings became Emperor until India was granted independence in 1947.

ORIGINS OF THE EMPIRE

The British Empire dates from the time of Elizabeth I and began almost by chance; certainly no grand plan of world domination was ever openly conceived by any one monarch. In Elizabeth's time, England was often at war with France and Spain, the two most powerful nations in Europe, which cut off our normal trade routes. New markets had to be found and so began a series of voyages of discovery to uncharted areas of the world where exotic foods were found and introduced to the English. The voyages began as mere piratical raids to steal riches from the Spanish colonies in South America, but they soon became serious quests for land and dominions, mostly along the eastern coast of North America.

DECLINE OF THE EMPIRE

The Empire probably reached its zenith and fullest extent in terms of both land mass and power at about 1920 when the former German colonies in Africa and Asia were taken over following the First World War. Eventually, resources were stretched too thinly for successful control of so large an empire. The military were unable to sustain the growth and when several countries expressed a wish to re-assert their own sovereignty, coupled with serious economic problems at home, the Empire began to break up and fall into decline.

EDWARD VII

BORN 1841 • ACCEDED 1901 • DIED 1910

SANDRINGHAM

The Norfolk estate of Sandringham has become a great, out-of-town favourite as a royal residence. It was purchased by Edward VII while he was still Prince of Wales in 1862 as a private residence. It consisted then of a large, neglected house and over 6,000 acres of land. Edward extended and improved the property considerably over the years and it is now often the centre of Christmas celebrations for the present royal family.

AUSTRALIA

Australia was granted dominion status in 1901, its people having long expressed a wish to be self-governing. Australia, although lightly populated by aboriginal natives, was largely an empty wilderness when it was added to the British Empire. Many new settlers were encouraged to move there to establish a proper, self-sufficient colony. Also, to help boost the population, many prisoners in England had their sentences commuted to transportation to the colonies, especially Australia.

dward VII was the eldest son of Queen Victoria and Prince Albert, though his relationship with his parents, especially his mother, was often strained. Even though he took over many of her administrative duties as Prince of Wales, she did not entirely trust his judgement and often excluded him from any real involvement in governmental matters. He lived life to the full (which earned him both popularity and derision) and had several mistresses, even though he was said to be happily married to Princess Alexandra, of Denmark, for many years.

THE BEGINNINGS OF THE WELFARE STATE

In 1887 the Independent Labour Party was founded, with the express intent of social reform, particularly for the downtrodden working

classes. Although they did not form their first government until 1924, they greatly influenced the other political parties, especially the Liberals, and pressed for several measures to eradicate social evils. Between 1906-09 a number of reforms were introduced, including labour exchanges for the unemployed and free school meals for the poor. Old-age pensions were introduced in 1908 for all people over 70.

1901	**1901**	**1902**	**1903**	**1904**
Edward VII accedes to the throne.	*Marconi makes first trans-Atlantic radio transmission.*	*Robert Bosch invents the spark plug.*	*Emmeline Pankhurst founds the Women's Social and Political Union (known as the Suffragettes).*	*First escalator opens in Paris.*
1901	**1902**	**1903**		**1904**
Australia granted dominion status within the Empire.	*Order of Merit introduced.*	*The Wright brothers make the first manned flight.*		*Britain and France sign the Entente Cordiale.*

🏛 ARCHITECTURE   📖 ARTS & LITERATURE   ⌖ EXPLORATION   ⬥ FAMOUS BATTLES

EMMELINE PANKHURST

In 1903 Emmeline Pankhurst formed the Women's Social and Political Union (WSPU) to fight for women's rights. The crusade for women's rights had been in existence for some time and had won some victories, but in 1903 women were still not allowed to vote. Members of WSPU were known as 'suffragettes' and in 1908 over half a million women gathered at a rally in Hyde Park, known as Women's Sunday, to protest at the inequality of women's rights. Suffragettes, including Emmeline Pankhurst, were often arrested for demonstrating, eventually winning their rights in 1918, when all women over 30 were given the right to vote, extended in 1928 to all women over 21.

WRIGHT BROTHERS

The first powered flight in a 'heavier-than-air machine' (as opposed to balloon flight) was by the Americans Orville and Wilbur Wright in December 1903. Their biplane (called 'The Flier') took off from Kitty Hawk, in North Carolina, and was based on unpowered gliders developed by the German Otto Lilienthal some 10 years before.

ENTENTE CORDIALE

The historic 'Entente Cordiale' (or 'cordial understanding') was an agreement between Britain and France to settle territorial disputes, further extended in 1908 to include Russia ('the Triple Entente'). Edward had a great love of France and on a visit to Paris in 1903 he paved the way for the political discussions that followed. The major powers of Europe seemed to be on a collision course and the agreement was intended to settle land disputes and avert war by forming an opposing group to balance the power of the Triple Alliance between Germany, Italy and Austria-Hungary.

INDISCRETIONS

Edward spent so long in the wings waiting to be king that he spent most of his time socialising, enjoying the pomp and the ceremony that accompanies the crown. He was quite open about his many affairs and had liaisons with Lillie Langtry (right) and Sarah Bernhardt, both famous actresses of the time.

1905 First dial telephone invented.	**1907** New Zealand granted dominion status.	**1908** Triple Entente signed between Britain, France and Russia.	(as Chancellor) introduces the controversial 'People's Budget'.	English Channel. **1910** Parliament curbs the power of the House of Lords.
1905 Completion of the electrification of London's underground.	**1908** Henry Ford introduced the Model-T car.	**1909** Lloyd-George	**1909** Louis Blériot flies single-winged aircraft across	**1910** Edward VII dies.

GOVERNMENT   HEALTH & MEDICINE   JUSTICE   RELIGION   SCIENCE

GEORGE V
BORN 1865 • ACCEDED 1910 • DIED 1936

As has so often been the case with the British monarchy, George V was not born to be king and only acceded to the throne because of the death of his brother, Edward. His reign was one of great turbulence, marked by social unrest, a world war and changes to the constitution which curbed the powers of the House of Lords. George V made the first Christmas broadcast to the nation to try to lift the people's spirits, a tradition still performed by the ruling monarch today.

RUSSIAN REVOLUTION

George V's cousin was Nicholas II, Tsar of Russia. Revolution broke out in Russia in 1917, resulting in the abdication of the Tsar, who, along with his family, was murdered soon afterwards by the Bolsheviks. The story of the revolution is a complex one. It began in 1905 following a disastrous war between Russia and Japan. The Tsar agreed to certain concessions and peace prevailed, but when these were withdrawn in 1917, revolution erupted again. The Tsar was forced to abdicate and a western-style liberal republican government was formed, but this was itself overthrown eight months later by the Bolsheviks, a socialist group led by Lenin. The revolution itself had been comparatively bloodless, but the civil war that ensued between the counter-revolutionary 'white' Russians and the 'red' Russians led by Trotsky, led to an estimated six million Russians losing their lives.

TITANIC SINKS

In April 1912 the 'SS Titanic' set sail on her maiden voyage from Britain to America. The ship was then the biggest ever built and was claimed to be unsinkable. It struck an iceberg in bad weather a few days later and sank within hours. Because insufficient lifeboats were provided, 1513 of the original 2224 passengers drowned. The wreck was discovered in 1980 and subsequently explored and photographed. An exhibition was mounted at the National Maritime Museum in Greenwich in 1995 of artefacts retrieved from the wreck.

1910 George V accedes to the throne.	Act provides financial benefits for the sick and unemployed.	**1914** The church in Wales is disestablished.	**1914** Battle of Ypres	**1916** David Lloyd George becomes Prime Minister.
1911 Parliament Act issued.	**1912** The Titanic sinks on her maiden voyage.	**1914** The 1st World War breaks out.	**1915** Gallipoli expedition fails.	**1917** Russian Revolution breaks out.
1911 National Insurance			**1916** Battle of the Somme	

ARCHITECTURE   ARTS & LITERATURE   EXPLORATION   FAMOUS BATTLES

GENERAL STRIKE

In May 1926 Britain was subjected to a General Strike. It had been caused by a growing crisis in the mining industry. When miners were asked to work longer hours for less money, they came out on strike, supported by an estimated 90% of all workers in Britain, bringing the country to a virtual standstill. The government had anticipated the strike and instigated various interim measures, including use of the military for essential services. The Trades Union Congress (TUC) negotiated a return to work after just nine days, having failed to get their demands met. The miners felt betrayed and stayed out on strike for a further six months, until starvation forced them to accept defeat. Shown above is a policeman protecting a strike-breaking bus driver.

GREAT DEPRESSION

The reasons for the Great Depression (or prolonged economic slump), that hit most countries in the western world, are obviously complex, but they basically stem from the economic downturn following the First World War, which was a financial drain on all participating countries. The Depression hit Britain in 1929 and by 1930 unemployment had reached over three million.

IRELAND DIVIDED

Protestant English settlers moved to Ireland in Tudor times, particularly around the Ulster area. The Irish Parliament came to be dominated by Protestants and the Catholics, who were the majority, became second class citizens. In 1920-22 failure to resolve the problems in Ireland resulted in an agreement to partition the country. The six counties of Ulster became the province of Northern Ireland and remained part of the United Kingdom, while the remaining counties became known as Eire, the Free State of Ireland.

LLOYD GEORGE

David Lloyd George (First Earl of Dwyfor, 1863–1945) was one of the great orators of his time. Liberal M.P. for Caernarvon Boroughs between 1890-1945, he became Prime Minister of a coalition government between 1916-22.

🥄 NATIONAL HEALTH INSURANCE ACT

The National Insurance Act was passed in 1911 by Herbert Asquith's Liberal government, which gave manual workers and many other employees a small wage and free medical attention during periods of sickness. A small weekly insurance premium was collected from each worker, which was supplemented by the government. The Act, which also provided certain workers with unemployment pay and was extended in 1920 to most other workers, still forms the basis of the modern welfare state.

📜 REFORM ACT

The Reform Act of 1918 finally gave the vote to certain women over the age of 30 after years of campaigning by the suffragette movement. During the First World War many jobs normally done by men had to be performed by women which, indirectly, helped the suffragette cause.

📜 STATUTE OF WESTMINSTER

By George V's reign several countries in the British Empire, including Canada, Australia and New Zealand, had received dominion status and in 1931 their independence was recognised by the Statute of Westminster. Although still part of the British Commonwealth and influenced by Britain, such countries became self-governing.

1918	**1919**	**1920/21**	**1928**	**1932**
1st World War ends.	Lady Astor becomes first	Ireland partitioned.	Right to vote	First Christmas
1918	woman M.P. in Britain.	**1926**	given to all	speech by the
Reform Act	**1919**	General Strike	women over 21.	reigning monarch.
gives votes to	Alcock and Brown fly non-	in support	**1931**	**1936**
women over 30.	stop across the Atlantic.	of coal miners.	Great Depression.	George V dies.

📜 GOVERNMENT   🥄 HEALTH & MEDICINE   ⚖️ JUSTICE   ✝ RELIGION   📏 SCIENCE

FIRST WORLD WAR
(1914-1918)

The underlying causes of the First World War are, even now, little understood in their entirety. Contrary to popular belief, it is unlikely that Germany was at that time making a bid for world domination. It began more as a trade war between the various powers of Europe, who all had colonies scattered around the world. Each country mistrusted the others and a series of alliances were drawn up to spread the balance of power and prevent any one country from becoming too powerful. What started out with Germany flexing its muscles to protect its dominions and bullying its near neighbours into submission, soon escalated into first, Europe-wide, and then world-wide warfare.

THE KAISER (1859–1941)

The Kaiser, Wilhelm II, was Queen Victoria's grandson and George V's cousin, though George fully supported the government's stand against the Germans when they invaded Belgium in 1914. Wilhelm was German Emperor and King of Prussia between 1888-1918. He was forced to abdicate after the war and fled to the Netherlands in exile until his death.

THE WAR BEGINS

The spark that began the conflict occurred in 1914 when the heir to the Austrian throne, Archduke Franz Ferdinand, was assassinated. The Austrians blamed the Serbians and declared war on them. Russia rushed to Serbia's aid and Germany to Austria's. Britain became involved when Germany invaded Belgium, which had been neutral until then, posing a threat to Britain's maritime security.

TRENCH WARFARE

Trench warfare, a comparatively new innovation, dominated the military strategies of the First World War. The digging of trenches by sappers and miners had long been known in siege operations, but here it became the dominant strategy following the deadlock after the Battle of Ypres. Thousands of soldiers were forced to live in the trenches, drawn up by each side along the battle lines, often for months at a time. Conditions were appalling and the loss of life was horrendous as periodically one side or the other would rush the trenches of the enemy to gain a few yards of territory.

ARCHITECTURE   ARTS & LITERATURE   EXPLORATION   FAMOUS BATTLES

JOIN TOGETHER
TRAIN TOGETHER
EMBARK TOGETHER
FIGHT TOGETHER

LIEUT. JACKA V.C.

Enlist in the Sportsmen's Thousand

SHOW THE ENEMY WHAT AUSTRALIAN SPORTING MEN CAN DO.

VOLUNTEERS SIGN UP

The allied army consisted largely of untrained civilians. Mounting unemployment at home meant that there was no shortage of volunteers to sign up for military service in Europe. Creative advertisements were used to encourage young men in particular to join up. The average age of recruits was just 19. The conflict was said to be the war to end all wars and was expected to be over in just six weeks.

PEACE TREATY

Following the German defeat in the Marne, the Kaiser left Germany for Holland. Germany formally surrendered on 11th November 1918 and signed armistice agreements dictated by the allies, marking the end of what was probably the bloodiest and most titanic conflict ever fought. Germany was disarmed and forbidden to re-arm, in addition to being presented with a huge bill for war damage, but later ignored both of these terms. The Peace Treaty of Versailles (below) in 1919 (and others) redrew the map of the world, dividing up the German colonies and the old Austro-Hungarian Empire among the allies. Several entirely new European states were thus created and a League of Nations formed to prevent such a war happening again.

DOG FIGHT

A new form of warfare emerged in the First World War, that of attack from the air. Britain suffered 52 air raids between 1914-18, killing over 500 people. Bombs were dropped mostly from huge gas filled airships, protected by fighter planes. By the end of the war Britain had the largest air force in the world. One-to-one 'dog-fights' become a common occurrence.

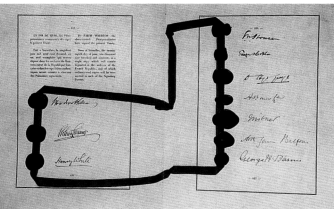

GOVERNMENT   HEALTH & MEDICINE   JUSTICE   RELIGION   SCIENCE

POPULAR PRINCE

As Prince of Wales, Edward was popular with the people. He visited America on several occasions. He was happiest when socialising and disliked the pomp and ceremony that accompanied royal occasions, which endeared him to the people, but infuriated his father.

MRS. SIMPSON

Mrs. Wallis Warfield Simpson was an American, who had already divorced one husband and was in the process of divorcing her second, when she met Prince Edward in 1931. The two soon fell in love, sparking off a constitutional crisis. At that time the Church of England refused to bless the marriage of divorcees, which made her an unsuitable candidate for a queen. Once King, Edward would also be head of the English Church, which made the dilemma more than just a personal problem.

CRYSTAL PALACE BURNS DOWN

Joseph Paxton's masterpiece in glass and iron, the Crystal Palace, accidentally burned down in 1936. This incredible building had been erected in Hyde Park in 1851 for the Great Exhibition and had already survived a move to Sydenham, in south London, when it was carefully dismantled and re-erected at its new site. Parts of the building had been let out and it is believed a spark from electrical equipment ignited the accumulated dust in the cellars and set fire to the building. The blaze, which quickly took hold, could be seen for miles around.

● SPANISH CIVIL WAR

In 1923 a military coup by Miguel Rivera and the Spanish Nationalists ousted the democratic government of Spain, assisted by the fascist states of Italy and Nazi Germany. Between 1930-31 Rivera's government was itself overthrown by Republicans, who won the general election in 1936. Civil war broke out the same year between the Republicans and the Nationalists, under General Franco. The civil war came to an end in 1939 with General Franco being declared dictator, a position he held until his death in 1975. In that year, King Juan Carlos I became the new head of state, followed two years later by the first free elections since 1936.

🬠 FIRST TELEVISION BROADCAST

Television is a direct extension of radio and was pioneered by the Scottish inventor John Logie Baird. He first demonstrated the use of television broadcasts in 1925. The first television service in the world was broadcast by the B.B.C. in 1936, though it was another 30 years before television became a common feature in most households.

1936
Edward VIII accedes to the throne.

1936
Spanish Civil War breaks out.

Britain re-arms in preparation for another war.

1936
The Supermarine Spitfire makes its maiden flight.

1936
First train ferry service across English Channel.

1936
Jean Batten flies solo from Britain to New Zealand.

1936
Hitler rebuilds the German armed forces and

1936
The Crystal Palace burns down.

1936
First television service in the world by the B.B.C.

1936
Edward VIII abdicates.

106

🏛 ARCHITECTURE   📖 ARTS & LITERATURE   ⚑ EXPLORATION   ● FAMOUS BATTLES

EDWARD VIII

BORN 1894 • ACCEDED 1936 • ABDICATED 1936 • DIED 1972

Edward VIII acceded to the throne on 29th January 1936, but ruled for just 325 days, abdicating the throne on 11th December later the same year. He was created Duke of Windsor soon after his abdication, a title he held until his death, in self-imposed exile in France, in 1972. His relationship with his father, George V, had always been strained. George is reported to have said that Edward would ruin himself within a year of succeeding to the throne, little realising the prophetic truth of his statement.

OUTSPOKEN VIEWS

Edward was noted for being somewhat headstrong and for holding outspoken and sometimes controversial views. On one occasion, while visiting Wales as king (one of his few public engagements) he embarrassed the government by saying that something should be done to reduce unemployment and he even contributed towards the miners' relief fund during the General Strike. He is also known to have held certain sympathies with Germany during the Second World War.

EXILE IN FRANCE

Edward's decision to abdicate, although received with sympathy by the general population, met with grave disapproval by members of the royal family, many of whom disowned him and refused to acknowledge Mrs. Simpson. Edward waited until after his brother Albert's coronation as George VI the following year before he married. The wedding ceremony was held at Chateau de Cande, near Tours, in France, on 3rd June 1937. They withdrew completely from public life and Edward died in exile on 18th May 1972.

THE KING ABDICATES

The Prime Minister, Stanley Baldwin, made the government's position crystal clear. Neither the monarchy nor the Church could be brought into disrepute and so Edward had to choose between the crown and Mrs. Simpson. The King decided that he did not want to continue ruling without Wallis as his queen and so chose to abdicate the crown. He did so on 11th December 1936, before he had been crowned. A formal 'Instrument of Abdication' was drawn up by Baldwin, which was rushed through Parliament. The following day Edward spoke to the public on the radio as a private citizen, giving the heartfelt reasons for his decision.

L'illustré du Petit Journal
50 centimes
DIMANCHE 23 MAI 1937

Le duc de WINDSOR et Mrs WARFIELD vivent dans le château de Candé leurs derniers jours de fiançailles avant la célébration de leur mariage
(voir l'article page 7)

GOVERNMENT   HEALTH & MEDICINE   JUSTICE   RELIGION   SCIENCE

GEORGE VI

BORN 1895 • ACCEDED 1936 • DIED 1952

LADY ELIZABETH BOWES-LYON

George married Lady Elizabeth Bowes-Lyon in 1923 and together they had two daughters. A devoted wife and mother, Elizabeth soon became a firm royal favourite with the British public. When George died unexpectedly at the comparatively young age of 56, she continued to offer her support to the young Queen Elizabeth II and she carried out several public duties each year until her death in 2002.

FAMILY MAN

George became one of our most popular monarchs, due in no small part to his lack of pretension. Aware of his own shortcomings, he strove hard to overcome his stammer so that he could perform his duties with dignity. Always a very private, family man, he moved his family into the Royal Lodge in the grounds of Windsor Castle. This, coupled with his decision to remain in Britain throughout the War, endeared him to the public.

When Edward VIII abdicated in 1936 the crown passed to George V's second son, Albert, who assumed the name George VI on his coronation. Another monarch not groomed for kingship, he was an intensely shy man, nervous in public, and suffered from an acute stammer. He is said to have confessed to his cousin, Lord Louis Mountbatten, 'I never wanted this to happen. I'm only a naval officer, it's the only thing I know about'. Nevertheless, George proved himself more than equal to the task, especially during the War years.

VISITING THE TROOPS

George refused to leave England during the Second World War, even after Buckingham Palace was bombed in 1940, and made several morale-boosting visits to the troops abroad. He also wanted to take a more active role in the war effort, though he was dissuaded from doing so by Winston Churchill, the Prime Minister. He instigated the George Cross and the George Medal, awarded to recognise civilian heroism. In 1942 the George Cross was awarded to the entire population of Malta in recognition of their brave resistance to a massive German onslaught.

INDIA GIVEN INDEPENDENCE

Most of the member states of the Empire sent troops to help with Britain's war effort. When the war was over, one of the principal effects was to strengthen the resolve of nationalism within the Empire, especially in the Near and Far East, where a bitter struggle for independence had been going on for some years. Supported by the new Labour government, legislation was passed in 1947 to give Burma, India, Pakistan and Ceylon independence, making them self-governing dominions of the British Commonwealth. Here we can see Gandhi being arrested in 1932 for his civil disobedience tactic.

1936 Edward's younger brother Albert accedes to the throne as George VI.	**1940** The 'Mallard' sets all-time speed record for steam train at 126 m.p.h. **1939** 2nd World War	breaks out. **1940** Dunkirk - evacuation of allied troops from beaches' of northern France.	**1940** Winston Churchill becomes Prime Minister. **1940** Battle of Britain fought in skies over southern	England, German defeat halts invasion of Britain. **1941** U.S.A. enters war following Japanese bombing of Pearl Harbour.

🏛 ARCHITECTURE   📖 ARTS & LITERATURE   ⚑ EXPLORATION   💣 FAMOUS BATTLES

NATIONAL HEALTH SERVICE

When the Second World War ended, a growing wish for social change swept the country. Many people were tired of the old ways and wanted something new. The Labour Party won a sensational victory in the 1945 election and within three years radical social changes were introduced. Between 1946-48 the National Insurance, Assistance and Health Service Acts were passed, which provided for a free health service for all, based on equality rather than on an ability to pay. Sickness, unemployment and pension payments were also significantly revised and several key, but ailing industries, such as the railways, gas and electric companies, were nationalised.

UNITED NATIONS FORM

The United Nations was formed in 1945 immediately after the end of the Second World War. The original Charter was drawn up by the Allied Powers to preserve world peace and security, to encourage nations to be just towards one another, to help nations co-operate in solving their problems and to act as an agency through which all nations could work together to achieve these goals. The General Assembly of the United Nations meets annually in New York.

FESTIVAL OF BRITAIN

In the years after the Second World War the government, with the full support of George, decided to hold a huge festival to boost morale and give the people hope for a brighter future. The Festival of Britain was held in 1951, on the centenary of the Great Exhibition of 1851. Concentrating on Britain's artistic achievements, the festival was a great success and included the building of the Festival Hall on the Embankment.

CORONATION MUG

Since the 18th century it has been fashionable for china and porcelain manufacturers to produce commemorative pieces to celebrate significant royal occasions, such as coronations, weddings and jubilees. Such pieces have since become collectors' items. This decorative mug was produced to mark the coronation of George VI in May 1937.

LA DOMENICA DEL CORRIERE

1942	1945	1947	1949	1951
Kodak introduces colour print film.	End of 2nd World War.	India partitioned and granted independence.	Boeing Superfortress makes first non-stop flight around the world.	Winston Churchill becomes Prime Minster again.
1944	**1945**	**1948**	**1951**	**1952**
D-Day landings in Normandy.	United Nations founded to promote world peace.	National Health Service formed.	Festival of Britain.	George VI dies.

GOVERNMENT • HEALTH & MEDICINE • JUSTICE • RELIGION • SCIENCE

WINSTON CHURCHILL
(1874–1965)

Probably the greatest wartime leader this country has ever seen, Sir Winston Churchill was born at Blenheim Palace in 1874. He began his somewhat chequered career as a newspaper correspondent during the Boer War. He became a Conservative M.P. in 1900, joined the Liberals in 1904 and changed back to the Tories in 1929. When Neville Chamberlain resigned in 1940 he became the Prime Minister of a coalition government for the remainder of the War and again between 1951-55 as a Conservative. Also a writer and painter of some repute, he won the Nobel Prize for Literature in 1953.

SECOND WORLD WAR
(1939–1945)

The reasons for the outbreak of the Second World War are much easier to understand than those for the First World War and grew directly, as a natural consequence, from the first world conflict. Following that war the blight of economic recession fell upon the whole of Europe. It affected Germany harder because it had been presented with a massive compensation bill to cover the cost of repairing the damage of war. Unemployment and inflation ran unchecked and the resulting sense of grievance paved the way for social unrest. When the fanatical Adolf Hitler appeared on the scene, inciting the people with his powerful speeches of world domination, he won a lot of support. Having already flouted the Treaty of Versailles by building up the German army, when he invaded Poland on 1st September 1939 Britain and France were drawn into events. War was declared on Germany on 3rd September 1939.

D-DAY LANDINGS

At dawn on 6th June 1944 the Allies began their decisive push back against the Germans, beginning with the invasion of France. The Germans had built a chain of fortifications along the Channel shore and made all the ports impregnable from attack. On that day a series of landings began on the beaches of Normandy, known as 'Operation Overlord'. Altogether some 5000 ships carried over 300,000 men, 54,000 vehicles and 100,000 tons of supplies to France, protected by 10,000 warplanes. What made the invasion possible was a British invention called 'Mulberries', or floating harbours, which enabled the Allies to bypass the German-held Channel ports.

END OF HOSTILITIES

At the end of the First World War over 10 million people had been killed, most of them military personnel. The final death toll after hostilities ended in the Second World War was much higher because of civilian casualties, and exceeded 40 million. The war in Europe ended on 8th May 1945 when Germany surrendered unconditionally. The war dragged on in the Pacific a little longer because Japan refused to give up the fight. In August, however, America dropped two atomic bombs on Japanese cities, causing unprecedented damage. On 14th August Japan also surrendered. The Second World War was over.

PRINCESS ELIZABETH

During the War George VI made several morale-boosting trips abroad to visit the troops. Although only 13 when war was declared, the young Princess Elizabeth continued her father's personal involvement in the war effort by signing up with the Auxiliary Transport Service on her 18th birthday, which won great public acclaim.

DUNKIRK

After just eight months of the war Hitler's superior army (in terms of both size and equipment) swept across northern Europe, cutting off the allied Anglo-French-Belgian forces. The Belgians surrendered, leaving the French and British hemmed in around the Channel port of Dunkirk. What followed was little short of a miracle. Under heavy cloud cover, which protected them from aerial attack, a convoy of British naval and merchant ships, supported by a flotilla of tugs, yachts, fishing boats, barges, (indeed anything that could make the journey) somehow managed to evacuate the bulk of the army (some 338,000) back to England, and safety.

WOMEN'S LAND ARMY

Unlike any other war in history, the Second World War directly affected the lives of civilians at home as much as the troops fighting on the front. Women were employed to do many of the jobs formerly done by men (who were forced to join the services) including munitions and farm work. The latter became known affectionately as the 'Women's Land Army'.

ADOLF HITLER (1889-1945)

Born in Austria, Adolf Hitler served as a corporal in the German army during World War I. He became leader of the extreme right-wing Nationalist Socialist Party (Nazi) in 1920 and three years later attempted, unsuccessfully, to overthrow the government. During his subsequent term in prison he wrote the political treatise '*Mein Kampf*', in which he outlined his intentions to control Europe. On his release he returned to politics and won the parliamentary election in 1930, becoming chancellor in 1933. He is believed to have committed suicide after the fall of Berlin in 1945.

THE BATTLE OF BRITAIN

The Battle of Britain was the first major battle to be fought solely in the air. It began in July 1940 shortly after France had fallen to the Germans, when Hitler launched operation 'Sealion', the invasion of Britain. To establish air supremacy, which Hitler needed to launch his invasion plans, the German Luftwaffe fought it out with the R.A.F. over the skies of south-east England for the next two months. The supremacy of the Spitfires and Hurricanes over the German Messerschmitt 109s eventually won the battle. Losses were heavy (in August alone, over 300 of the 1,400 British pilots were killed) but Hitler accepted defeat and called off the invasion on 17th September.

U.S.A. ENTERS THE WAR

Japan joined forces with Germany and Italy against the allied forces of Europe. On 7th December 1941 America was brought into the conflict when the U.S. fleet was subjected to an unprovoked and quite devastating attack on the naval base at Pearl Harbor, in Hawaii.

📜 GOVERNMENT   🥣 HEALTH & MEDICINE   ⚖️ JUSTICE   ✟ RELIGION   🗲 SCIENCE

⚑ SPACE TRAVEL

Towards the end of the Second World War a great deal of research was carried out on rocket development, which was later put to use in the American and Russian space programmes. The first communications satellite (Sputnik) was put into space by the Russians in 1957, followed by the first manned space flight by Yuri Gagarin in 1961. On 20th July 1969 the U.S.A. succeeded in launching the first manned space flight (Apollo 11) to land on the moon.

☀ FIRST GULF WAR

On 2nd August 1990 the President of Iraq, Saddam Hussein, invaded neighbouring Kuwait, having failed to reach an agreement over oil prices. Days later, the U.N. imposed economic sanctions on Iraq and on 29th November they passed a resolution authorising the use of military force to liberate Kuwait. A brief, high-technology war ensued, resulting in an allied victory, headed by America and Britain. Kuwait was liberated in February 1991, followed by a ceasefire in April. A U.N. peacekeeping force was afterwards sent to Iraq.

MARGARET THATCHER

Margaret Thatcher became Britain's first woman Prime Minister in 1979 when she swept to power under the Conservative Party. Always a controversial figure, she proved also to be one of our ablest administrators and is generally regarded as lifting Britain out of recession, though her policies were often seen as overly harsh. She suffered a somewhat ignominious end to a glittering political career when, in 1990, she was ousted as head of the Conservative Party by her fellow politicians.

BRITAIN JOINS E.E.C.

The European Economic Community, now simply the European Community (E.C.), was formed in 1957 by the Treaty of Rome. Known as the Common Market, it was founded in post-war Europe to provide economic security to its member states by working collectively to support one another. Britain applied for membership several times before finally being accepted in 1973.

POLL TAX REINTRODUCED

In 1989 the Conservative government of the day, under Margaret Thatcher, attempted to reintroduce the Poll Tax (known as the Community Charge) which levied a local council tax across the board, regardless of an individual's ability to pay. It met with widespread revolt from the public and many people were taken to court for non-payment. It proved as unsuccessful as the first attempt to introduce the tax in 1381, which led to the Peasants' Revolt on that occasion. The tax was withdrawn and replaced with the current Council Tax system.

1952 Elizabeth II accedes to the throne.	**1953** First hovercraft built in Britain.	**1959** Discovery of oil in the North Sea.	*for the first time.* **1965** Sir Winston Churchill dies.	**1969** First manned space flight lands on the moon.
1953 Edmund Hillary conquers Mount Everest.	**1955** Churchill resigns as Prime Minister.	**1962** The Beatles enter the British music charts	**1969** Prince Charles invested as Prince of Wales.	**1969** 'Concord' makes its maiden flight.

🏛 **ARCHITECTURE**   📖 **ARTS & LITERATURE**   ⚑ **EXPLORATION**   ☀ **FAMOUS BATTLES**

ELIZABETH II

BORN 1926 • ACCEDED 1952

lizabeth came to the throne at the age of 25 on the unexpected death of her father. One of only a handful of queens to rule Britain, she has become a firm favourite with the public and restored much of the popularity of the monarchy. Although her official duties are limited, she still officially presides at the state opening of Parliament and remains supreme head of the British armed services. Elizabeth married Philip Mountbatten in 1947 (who then became Duke of Edinburgh) and together they have had four children.

THE FUTURE OF THE MONARCHY

Given the present minimalist influence over affairs of state, it would seem probable that Britain will continue to preserve its monarchy. There are no great movements afoot to abolish the monarchy, though it has fallen in popularity in recent years. The Royal family is constantly in the public eye, both at home and abroad. Their charity work, family disputes and wide-varying press coverage keeps the future of the monarchy a constant topic of conversation.

THE PEOPLE'S PRINCESS

On 31st August 1997, Princess Diana (the mother of the future king - Prince William) suffered a fatal car crash on the streets of Paris. Although losing her royal status after her divorce from Prince Charles, she was always revered as the 'People's Princess', notably for her charitable work. Her early death sent shockwaves throughout the world and established her as a genuine world icon. Over 2.5 billion people watched her funeral – the largest television audience for a single event.

📖 THE SWINGING 60s

In the post-war years, a social revolution swept the Western world. Young people were no longer prepared to accept the values of their forefathers without question. A generation of rebels established new movements, particularly in art and music. The movement began with the new rock and roll music of America, but in the 1960s it was Britain that led the way. The most influential popular musical group of the time were the Beatles, still widely enjoyed today.

💣 FALKLANDS WAR

In 1982 a military junta in Argentina invaded the Falkland Islands and South Georgia, a self-governing British dependency in the South Atlantic, off the Argentina coast. The Argentinians seized control, even though the islands (known to them as the Islas Malvinas) had never been Argentinian territory. Britain sent a task force, headed by the largest fleet massed by this country since the Second World War. After a brief two month war, Britain emerged victorious, though not without a considerable struggle.

1971	1973	1979	1989	1997
Britain adopts decimal currency.	B.B.C. introduce teletext.	Sony first introduce the 'Walkman' personal stereo player.	Poll Tax reintroduced; leads to mass riots and is withdrawn.	Tories lose general election to Labour, ending a record 18 years in power.
1973 Britain joins the E.E.C. (the Common Market).	**1979** Margaret Thatcher becomes first woman Prime Minister.	**1982** The Falklands War.	**1991** The First Gulf War.	

📜 GOVERNMENT ⚗ HEALTH & MEDICINE ⚖ JUSTICE ✝ RELIGION 🎵 SCIENCE

The Windsors

THE SCOTTISH MONARCHY
(843–1214)

*T*he early years of the monarchy in Scotland, between the years 843–1034, roughly correspond to the period in England when the kings of the seven kingdoms of the Heptarchy jostled for power. The Scots, Angles, Picts and Celts were involved in a similar struggle in Scotland. The first king of a united Scotland was Kenneth MacAlpin, a Scot, from whom all the later kings of Scotland claimed to be descended.

DUNCAN I (1034–40)

Duncan I succeeded to the throne in 1034 and unsuccessfully launched an invasion of England in 1040. A civil war broke out in Scotland afterwards, during which Duncan was killed. He was succeeded by his cousin, Macbeth.

YEARS OF TURMOIL

Following the death of Malcolm III in 1093 Scotland underwent a period of considerable change and unrest, coinciding with a Norman invasion from England. Throughout this period, each of the next four Scottish kings tried to counter this invasion by re-asserting their claim to the northernmost counties of England as part of Scotland. Coupled with civil war and a growing period of social unrest, these were turbulent times indeed for Scotland. Malcolm III was succeeded by his brother Donald III in 1093. The following year he was overthrown by his nephew, who had himself crowned as Duncan II. Later that same year he was killed in battle and Donald III returned to the throne, only to be driven off again, on this occasion by Edgar, Duncan's half-brother, in 1097. Edgar ruled until 1107 when he was succeeded by his brother, who became Alexander I.

DAVID I (1124–54)

David succeeded his brother, Alexander I, to the throne in 1124. His long rule of 30 years established a sense of stability to the Scottish throne and he became one of Scotland's ablest rulers. He invited a number of prominent Normans to settle in Scotland and continued to introduce feudalism, although the system of government was never fully adopted in Scotland. A pious man, he founded several abbeys and tried unsuccessfully to invade England, being defeated by Stephen at the Battle of the Standard in 1138. David died in 1154 and was succeeded by his grandson, Malcolm IV.

ARCHITECTURE   ARTS & LITERATURE   EXPLORATION   FAMOUS BATTLES

MALCOLM III (1057–93)

Malcolm III took the throne after killing his second cousin, Macbeth. He married Edmund Ironside's granddaughter, Margaret, who was responsible for reforming the Scottish church. William I of England invaded Scotland in 1071–2 and introduced many feudal ideals and forced Malcolm to pay homage to him. Malcolm responded by invading England in 1093 in an attempt to annexe the three northernmost counties to Scotland, but he was killed in the attempt.

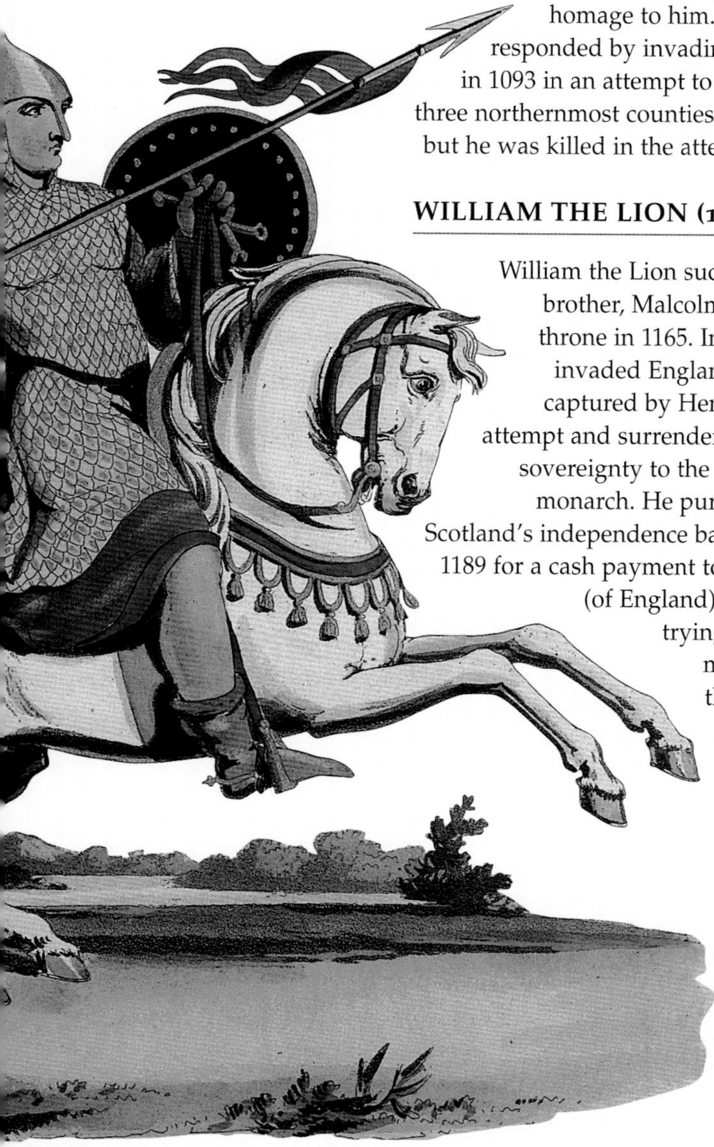

WILLIAM THE LION (1165–1214)

William the Lion succeeded his brother, Malcolm IV, to the throne in 1165. In 1173-74 he invaded England but was captured by Henry II in the attempt and surrendered Scottish sovereignty to the English monarch. He purchased Scotland's independence back again in 1189 for a cash payment to Richard I (of England) who was trying to raise money for the crusades. He died in 1214.

LINE OF SUCCESSION

Early Kings of Scotland

Kenneth MacAlpin - 843-859
Donald I - 859-863
Constantine I - 863-877
Aedh - 877-878
Eocha - 878-889
Donald II - 889-900
Constantine II - 900-942
Malcolm I - 942-954
Indulphus - 954-962
Dubf - 962-967
Cuilean - 967-971
Kenneth II - 971-995
Constantine III - 995-997
Kenneth III - 997-1005
Malcolm II - 1005-1034
Duncan I - 1034-1040
Macbeth - 1040-1057
Malcolm III - 1057-1093
Donald III - 1093-1094 & 1094-1097
Duncan II - 1094
Edgar - 1097-1107
Alexander I - 1107-1124
David I - 1124-1154
Malcolm IV - 1154-1165
William the Lion - 1165-1214

MACBETH (1040–57)

Macbeth came to the throne in 1040 on the death of his cousin, Duncan I. Although implicated with Duncan's death by Shakespeare, there is little evidence to support the claim. It should be pointed out that the 'Duncan' and 'Macbeth' of Shakespeare's play are largely fictitious characters and are not the real kings mentioned here. Macbeth was an able ruler who was killed by Malcolm, Duncan's son, at the Battle of Lumphanan.

GOVERNMENT   HEALTH & MEDICINE   JUSTICE   RELIGION   SCIENCE

SCOTTISH KINGS & QUEENS

(1214–1329)

Ever since William I's invasion of Scotland in 1071, when Malcolm III swore fealty to him as overlord, Scotland had fiercely fought for independence from England. In 1189 Richard I gave Scotland its freedom in return for a large cash payment to help fund his crusade to the Holy Land and in 1217 a peace treaty was signed between England and Scotland acknowledging Scotland's independence. Matters came to a head again in 1290 when the infant Margaret, the Maid of Norway and successor to the Scottish throne, died unexpectedly, opening the way for Edward I of England to re-assert his claim to Scotland.

ALEXANDER II
(1214–49)

When Alexander II ascended the Scottish throne in 1214 he was determined to rid the land of Viking invaders. Following several minor successes, in 1249 he tried an all-out assault, but died before the attack could be launched.

LINE OF SUCCESSION

Alexander II - 1214-49
Alexander III - 1249-86
Margaret of Norway - 1286-90
John Balliol - 1292-96
(Edward I of England ruled as king) 1296-1306
Robert I (Bruce) - 1306-29

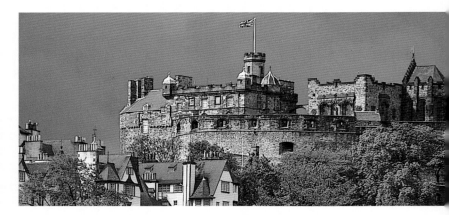

EDINBURGH CASTLE

Edinburgh Castle, home of the Scottish kings, towers 300ft. above the city. Castle Rock has been fortified since at least Iron Age times, though the medieval castle dates from about 1100. When Robert Bruce captured the castle from the English in 1313 he is said to have destroyed every building except the chapel. The castle, which has been largely rebuilt since then, contains part of the Scottish royal palace within its walls.

🏛 **ARCHITECTURE**   📖 **ARTS & LITERATURE**   🏴 **EXPLORATION**   💧 **FAMOUS BATTLES**

BATTLE OF BANNOCKBURN

This decisive battle between Scotland, under Robert Bruce, and England, under Edward II, took place near Stirling Castle on 23rd–24th June 1314. The Scots emerged victorious.

WILLIAM WALLACE

In 1295 John Balliol formed an alliance with France against England. The following year Edward I invaded Scotland, deposed Balliol and proclaimed himself King of Scotland. The Scots rebelled, led by William Wallace, who defeated Edward at the Battle of Stirling Bridge. In 1298 Edward re-invaded Scotland and defeated Wallace at the Battle of Falkirk. Wallace continued to lead the revolt against England until 1305, when he was betrayed and captured. He was found guilty of treason and was hanged, drawn and quartered.

THE STONE OF SCONE

Scottish monarchs were traditionally enthroned on this stone. In 1296 it was removed from Scone Abbey by Edward I to Westminster. It was returned in 1996 and can now be seen in Edinburgh Castle.

ALEXANDER III (1249–86)

Alexander III ascended the throne at just eight years old in 1249. He defeated the Vikings in 1263 and proved to be an able administrator. He died in an accident in 1286.

JOHN BALLIOL (1292–96)

In 1290 the Scottish throne fell vacant. A successor could not be agreed so Edward I of England was asked to mediate. He chose John Balliol, a weak man whom he thought he could manipulate.

ROBERT BRUCE (1306–29)

Following the execution of William Wallace in London, Robert Bruce declared himself leader of the rebels against English rule, even though he had originally offered his support to Edward. He was crowned King of Scotland as Robert I in 1306. The following year Edward re-invaded Scotland. Edward died en route but his invasion army forced Bruce into hiding. Bruce gradually gathered his strength and attacked Stirling Castle in 1314. Even after the English were defeated at Bannockburn, Scotland did not gain full independence. Bruce invaded England in 1327 and the following year Edward III signed the Treaty of Edinburgh, finally acknowledging Scotland's independence. Bruce died a year later.

GOVERNMENT   HEALTH & MEDICINE   JUSTICE   RELIGION   SCIENCE

🔥 BATTLE OF OTTERBURN

Richard II, of England, was a far less able king than his predecessor Edward III had been and in the border struggles between England and Scotland of the 14th century Scotland gained the upper hand. In 1388 Robert II defeated the English at the Battle of Otterburn.

ROBERT III (1390-1406)

When Robert II died the throne passed to his son John, who was crowned as Robert III. Curiously, although he had largely governed the country during his father's reign, when he himself became king he relinquished much of his power to his younger brother, Alexander. It was a period of excessive violence and near anarchy, when the Scottish monarchy turned to France yet again as an ally in its wars with England.

LINE OF SUCCESSION

David II (Bruce) - 1329-32 & 1341-71
Edward Balliol - 1332-41
Robert II - 1371-90
Robert III - 1390-1406

TREATY OF BERWICK

In 1346 David II invaded England but was defeated at Neville's Cross and confined to the Tower of London for 11 years. He was finally released in 1357 on signing the Treaty of Berwick in which he agreed to pay a huge ransom to Edward III of England, payable by instalments. Unable to make his payments, in 1363 David offered his throne to Edward III if he agreed to cancel the debt, but the Scottish parliament refused to sanction such a deal, stating that they would prefer to bankrupt the country rather than give in to such treachery by David.

EDWARD BALLIOL (1332-41)

In 1332 John Balliol's son, Edward, entered into an alliance with Edward III, of England. David II was driven into exile and Edward was crowned king, but on condition that he handed over large tracts of lowland Scotland to the English king. In 1341 Balliol was overthrown and David II re-asserted his claim to the throne.

🏛 ARCHITECTURE   📖 ARTS & LITERATURE   🏳 EXPLORATION   🔥 FAMOUS BATTLES

SCOTTISH KINGS & QUEENS

1329–1406

he 14th century was a period of almost constant struggle in Scotland to maintain the right for independence. The border counties of both England and Scotland were often the scene of bloody skirmishes as each struggled for supremacy and the land often changed hands between the two countries. Scotland formed an uneasy alliance with France, England's age-old enemy, in its bid for independence, though the French were frequently far from happy with the situation, which often worked against their own plans. It was a period of social unrest, weak governance and violence as the Scottish lords also struggled among themselves for supremacy.

DAVID II (1329-32 & 1341-71)

Following the bitter struggles of Robert Bruce's reign to maintain Scottish independence, the reign of his son, David II, was a complete disappointment to the people of Scotland. Although a long reign, his rule was marked by weakness and treachery; he even tried to sell his sovereignty to Edward III of England.

CAPTURE OF PRINCE JAMES

In 1406 Henry IV of England captured the 12 year old Prince James, Robert III's son, and imprisoned him in the Tower of London. The news is said to have brought on Robert's premature death. James remained a prisoner for 18 years, Scotland being ruled by his uncle, the Duke of Albany, in his absence.

ROBERT II (1371-90)

When David II died in 1371 he was succeeded by his nephew, Robert Stewart (or Stuart). He was the High Steward of Scotland and Robert Bruce's grandson. He was also the first Stuart monarch, so beginning a new Scottish dynasty, though he was a weak king and left much of the business of government to his eldest son, John, Earl of Carrick.

GOVERNMENT   HEALTH & MEDICINE   JUSTICE   RELIGION   SCIENCE

STIRLING CASTLE

Although of much earlier foundation, the earliest part of Stirling Castle to survive dates from the 15th century, when the Stuarts converted it from a medieval fortress to a magnificent royal palace. Standing at the gateway to the Highlands, it was always considered the most vital possession during Scotland's wars of independence and changed hands more times than any other Scottish castle.

● BATTLE OF FLODDEN FIELD

When James IV invaded the north of England in 1513, Henry VIII sent a massive force against him. James, most of his nobility and many of the leading church dignitaries were all killed at the Battle of Flodden Field.

📖 FIRST PRINTING PRESS

The first printing press in Scotland was set up in 1507 by Andrew Myllar, under the patronage of James IV.

📖 UNIVERSITY CITIES

The early Stuart period was an age of great learning. Three universities were founded in Scotland at this time: at St. Andrews (in 1412); Glasgow (in 1450) and Aberdeen (in 1495).

JAMES I (1406-37)

James I was born in 1394 and, at the age of 12, was captured by pirates who then handed him over to Henry IV of England. Later that same year his father, Robert III, died. Despite succeeding to the throne in 1406 Henry IV held him prisoner in England for 18 years, Scotland being ruled in his absence by a regent, James's uncle, the Duke of Albany. In 1424 James was released from prison and returned to Scotland as king. During his confinement Albany had allowed many of the barons almost free rein to do as they wished and James immediately set about curbing their power. His actions won popular support, but not among the barons, who assassinated him in 1437.

JAMES III (1460-88)

When James II died unexpectedly in 1460, the throne passed to his nine year old son, James III, and Scotland was once again ruled by a regency. He assumed personal control in about 1470 but he lacked the military attributes of his father. James was a pious, well-educated man who preferred music and the arts to battle. In 1482 the border town of Berwick-upon-Tweed was lost (not for the first time) to England, but on this occasion it was to remain in English hands. James was assassinated shortly after the Battle of Sauchiebur in 1488.

Margaret of Denmark, James III's Queen.

JAMES IV (1488-1513)

James IV succeeded his father in 1488 and, like his three predecessors, was a great patron of the arts. He was also an able administrator and established Scotland as a truly united and independent nation. He built up the armed services, particularly the navy, and commissioned the 'Great Michael', which was then the largest warship in the world. In 1503 he married Margaret Tudor, Henry VII's (of England) daughter, thus briefly uniting the two countries. However, when Henry VIII invaded France in 1513 James invaded England in support of his French allies, but was killed in the process.

🏛 ARCHITECTURE   📖 ARTS & LITERATURE   ⚐ EXPLORATION   ● FAMOUS BATTLES

SCOTTISH KINGS & QUEENS

(1406–1513)

When David II died, he was succeeded by Robert Stewart, his nephew, who was the High Steward of Scotland and grandson of Robert Bruce. The family later adopted the French spelling of their name, Stuart. A powerful, ambitious family, they were also great patrons of the arts and brought Scotland to the forefront of artistic and cultural development in Europe.

JAMES II (1437-60)

James II succeeded his father in 1437 and continued the fight to quell the power of the lords, particularly in the Highlands and Isles. He fought valiantly to control the clans, particularly the Black Douglas family, who had become a law unto themselves. He finally defeated them in 1455. He was a great patron of learning and the arts and founded Glasgow University, meeting his untimely end during the siege of Roxburgh Castle in 1460 when a cannon exploded in his face.

THE ORKNEYS & SHETLANDS

Although many people regard the island groups of the Orkneys and Shetlands (right) as always having been part of Scotland, they were not in fact acquired by Scotland until 1472. Prior to that they belonged to Norway and are still proud of their strong Nordic ancestry.

LINE OF SUCCESSION

Early Stuarts (1406-1513)

James I   1406-1437
James II   1437-1460
James III   1460-1488
James IV   1488-1513

📜 GOVERNMENT   ⚗ HEALTH & MEDICINE   ⚖ JUSTICE   ✝ RELIGION   ▯ SCIENCE

SCOTTISH KINGS & QUEENS
(1513–1625)

ames V proved a competent ruler, but the reigns of Mary and her son James VI (see pages 72-73) were a sad reflection of the former greatness of earlier Stuart monarchs. The reign of James VI also witnessed the end of Scottish independence. Although a Scottish king inherited the English throne, power gradually seeped away from Edinburgh to London, until by 1707 Scotland had even lost the right to hold its own Parliament.

MARY (1542–67) (KNOWN AS QUEEN OF SCOTS)

Mary, like so many Scottish monarchs, was a mere infant (just one week old) when she acceded to the throne in 1542. In 1548 she was packed off to France to be brought up by her mother's family, leaving Scotland once again in the care of a regency. In 1558 she married the French Dauphin and became, briefly, queen of France when he became king as Francis II, but he died in 1560 and Mary returned to Scotland the following year. She then married her cousin Henry, Lord Darnley, and became embroiled in a plot (probably against her will) to seize the throne of England.

JOHN KNOX

John Knox was a Scottish scholar and Protestant preacher who rose to prominence in England during Henry VIII's reign. He fled to Europe in 1553 when the Catholic Mary Tudor ascended the English throne. He later returned to Scotland in 1559, assisted by Elizabeth I, and established a Protestant religion in Scotland. He died in 1572.

ARCHITECTURE   ARTS & LITERATURE   EXPLORATION   FAMOUS BATTLES

A MURDEROUS AFFAIR

In 1566 Mary's private secretary, David Rizzio, was murdered in front of her, suspected of being her lover. She was later implicated in her husband Darnley's death and was forced to abdicate by the Scottish nobles. In 1568 she fled to England where Elizabeth I held her prisoner for 19 years before finally signing her death warrant in 1587.

FOTHERINGHAY CASTLE

It is perhaps fitting that the scene of Mary Queen of Scots' execution should itself be reduced to fragmentary remains. Fotheringhay Castle, in Northamptonshire, dates from about 1100 but was rebuilt in the 14th century. It was in the great hall, now demolished, that the pathetic figure of Mary was beheaded in 1587. Her dog is said to have crouched in the skirts of her headless corpse after the event.

JAMES V (1513-42)

James V succeeded to the throne as a 17 month old child on the death of his father at Flodden Field in 1513. Again, Scotland was ruled by a regency during James's minority, the king eventually taking full control of government in 1528. He felt betrayed by the Scottish lords and ruled very much without their consent. He proved himself to be a strong and fair king who, like his predecessors, was also a great patron of the arts.

✝ THE SCOTTISH REFORMATION

The Scottish Reformation of the church took place in the remarkably short space of 20 years, from about 1540–60. The driving force behind the movement was John Knox, a somewhat fanatical Protestant who was greatly influenced by the French theologian John Calvin. A much stricter doctrine was adopted than that followed by the Church of England, leading to the foundation of the Presbyterian Church in Scotland. In 1560 the Reformation Parliament in Scotland decided that it should be a Protestant nation.

▤ COURT OF SESSION

Despite losing its independent monarchy and Parliament, Scotland has retained its own legal, educational and religious systems to the present day. In 1532 the Court of Session was founded as the central court for civil justice.

◉ BATTLE OF SOLWAY MOSS

In 1542 James V launched another unsuccessful invasion of England. He was defeated at the Battle of Solway Moss and died, of natural causes, a few weeks later.

LINE OF SUCCESSION

Later Stuarts (1513–1625)

James V 1513-1542
Mary 1542-1567
James VI 1567-1625
(James I of England)

SIEGE OF LONDONDERRY

Following James II's deposition in 1688 a Catholic rebellion broke out in an attempt to reinstate him on the throne. The following year the rebels landed in Ireland and laid siege to Londonderry, occupied by Protestant forces loyal to William III, who took cover within the city walls for 105 days before English forces put down the rebellion.

BATTLE OF THE BOYNE

After the failure of his army to take Londonderry, James II travelled south to Drogheda, to the area around the River Boyne. His forces again engaged William III's army (in July 1690) and again faced defeat. This time, however, James gave up the fight and fled to France in exile, where he remained until his death in 1701.

ACT OF UNION

The Act of Union between Britain and Ireland was passed in 1800, but government was still heavily biased in favour of the Protestants even though they were a minority. The movement for Irish Home Rule began to gather momentum, but two Bills (in 1886 and again in 1893) failed to become law. Subsequent English governments failed to resolve the problems in Ireland and in 1920 Ireland was partitioned. The Free State, known as Eire, became a self-governing republic and the six counties of Northern Ireland remained part of the United Kingdom, sharing the same constitutional monarchy as England, Wales and Scotland.

THE NORMANS

The English invasion of Ireland began in 1154–5 during the reign of Henry II. The church in Ireland, though Christian, refused to follow the doctrines of Rome so Pope Adrian IV gave authority to Henry to invade Ireland, annexe the country to England and bring the church into line with Rome. It was not until 1166, however, that Henry sent his first invasion force to Ireland, during a dispute between the Irish kings when one, Dermot MacMurrough, King of Leinster, asked the English king for help. In 1171 Henry himself headed an invasion force. The heavily armoured Normans quickly gained control and he declared himself Lord of Ireland. Later the same year he forced the Irish clergy to acknowledge the pope's authority.

IRELAND DIVIDED

Although there were long-standing divisions in Ireland for many centuries before England's intervention between the various tribes and kingdoms, the religious divisions between Catholic and Protestant, which have become so much a part of the 'troubles' in Ireland in recent years, stem directly from the Tudor period. It was at that time that the first Protestant settlers (known as 'planters') were encouraged to settle in Ireland to strengthen the English position against possible alliances between Ireland, Spain and France. Intermarriage between the settlers and the Irish people, coupled with the growth of Protestantism in general, have subsequently led to deep social divisions between the people of Ireland.

THE MONARCHY OF IRELAND

The story of the Irish monarchy is complex because, like its neighbours, England, Scotland and Wales, it was not unified as a single nation until quite late in its history. The situation was further complicated in Ireland, however, because of interference from England, which sought to annexe it and protect itself from attack. The result was that before Ireland could be properly unified under one king, English kings claimed sovereignty from the 12th century onwards, a situation that perhaps goes some way to explain the deep-rooted divisions within Ireland today.

EARLY IRISH KINGS

Ireland, like Wales, Scotland and ancient Britain, has a Celtic ancestry but, unlike them, was little influenced by Saxon raids (though it was subjected to Danish invasions in the 9th and 10th centuries). Traditionally, six kings ruled separate provinces of Ireland who each swore loyalty to a High King. Each of the kingdoms was further sub-divided into tribes, each with their own leader, also known as kings. The last High King of Ireland was Brian Boru (above), King of Munster, who died in 1014 whilst defending Ireland against the Danes. When he died the remaining kings of the provinces fought an ongoing and, ultimately, unresolved civil war to gain supremacy.

THE TUDORS

Although subsequent medieval monarchs retained an influence over Irish affairs, the country was never fully conquered and several of the Celtic Irish kings continued to rule in defiance of English authority. Many of the English and Norman barons sent to Ireland married Irish women and adopted Irish lifestyles. It was not until the Tudor period that the re-invasion of Ireland became a priority once more. To protect himself from an Irish alliance with France, Henry VIII put down several rebellions against English rule and declared himself king of Ireland in 1541. Elizabeth I (and several of the Stuart kings who followed her) later encouraged Protestant settlements in Ireland to strengthen the English position by granting Irish estates to English nobles.

'THE PALE'

Despite Henry VIII's grandiose claim to be king of Ireland and the subsequent settlements by Protestants under later monarchs (mostly in Ulster) the English never really had much more than a toe-hold in Ireland. Prior to Henry VIII's time, most of the English settlements were confined to Dublin and its surrounding area. It became known as 'the Pale' because of the earth and timber defence works erected around the settlements to ward off attacks by Irish clansmen.

WILLIAM OF ORANGE

In 1688 the English Parliament invited the Protestant Dutch ruler, William of Orange (the name of the Dutch royal house), to depose the Catholic king of England, James II, and rule in his place. He became William III and ruled with Mary II, James's daughter. Not everyone accepted him at first and many Catholics joined James II in his attempt to win back the crown. In Ireland, the Protestants sided with William, while the Catholics supported James.

GOVERNMENT   HEALTH & MEDICINE   JUSTICE   RELIGION   SCIENCE

INDEX

DID YOU KNOW?

• *Queen Victoria ruled the British Empire for 64 years, longer than any other monarch. She became queen in 1837, when her uncle King William IV died without an heir. During her reign, the British colonial empire was the richest in the world, owning one-fourth of the world's land and ruling more than one-fourth of the world's people.*

• *The British royal family changed their surname (last name) from Saxe-Coburg-Gotha to Windsor in 1917.*

• *George V was king of England from 1910 to 1936. Son of Edward VII, King of England, and Princess Alexandra of Denmark, he married Queen Mary of Teck (called May) in 1893. Known as the Sailor Prince, he had an active naval career and rose to the rank of vice admiral in 1903.*

• *This is a traditional aid used in UK schools to help students remember the order of British Monarchs from William the Conqueror on . . .*

Willie Willie Harry Stee
Harry Dick John Harry three;
One two three Neds, Richard two
Harrys four five six....then who?
Edwards four five, Dick the bad,
Harrys (twain), Ned six (the lad);
Mary, Bessie, James you ken,
Then Charlie, Charlie, James again...
Will and Mary, Anna Gloria,
Georges four, Will four Victoria;
Edward seven next, and then
Came George the fifth in nineteen ten;
Ned the eighth soon abdicated
Then George six was coronated;
After which Elizabeth
And that's all folks until her death.

ACKNOWLEDGEMENTS

This Series is dedicated to J. Allan Twiggs whose enthusiasm for British History has inspired these four books.
We would also like to thank: Graham Rich, Tracey Pennington, and Peter Done for their assistance.
A CIP catalogue record for this book is available from the British Library. ISBN 1 86007 531 2
Printed in China.

Acknowledgements: Picture Credits t=top, b=bottom, c=centre, l=left, r=right, OFC=outside front cover, IFC=inside front cover, IBC=inside back cover, OBC=outside back cover.

AKG, London: 49cr (Galleria dell' Accademia Florence), 101tr, 104tl, 110t, 110br. Ancient Art & Architecture Library: 6tl, 6c, 6bl, 7cl, 7cr, 10l, 12tl, 14l, 16bc, 17bl, 20tl, 25br, 28tl & bl, 29tl, 30cr, 31cr, 34tl, 35t, 37r & inset, 39bl (detail), 39t, 40tl, 41tl & tr, 45t, 46bl, 49t, 51tl, 56tr, 57t & b, 66, 73tr, 76tl, 81t, 85br, 86tl, 90t, 91b. Barnaby Picture Library: 102b, 109t, 112tl. Bridgeman Art Library: 7t, 8b, 13cl, 17tl, 18br, 19tl, 23t, 25t, 31t, 35r (detail), 36, 37t, 40b (detail), 41t, 41br, 42cl (detail), 44tl, 46tl (detail), br, 47t, 48tl, 52tr &cr, 53cl, 55tl & cr, 62 tr, 57t, 60t, 62tl, 63t & bc, 65tr, 70b, 72cl, 74bc, 75t, 85t, 87t, 86r, 91t, 97t, 101l & br, 112tr ('True Blue c Ruskin Spear 191101990). The British Library: 24b. E.T. Archive: 95t. Chris Fairclough/Image Select: 8c, 11tr, 13tr, 24t, 29br 34c, 39br, 45c, 49cl, 60b, 63cl, 71cl, 75cr. Fotomas Index: 14br. Glasgow Museums : The Stirling Maxwell Collection: 56. Hever Castle Ltd: 50cr. Hulton Getty Collection: 16tl, 55br, 60tl, 76cl, 77t. Image Select: 5cl, 15t, 22tl, 104c, 105t, bl, br. Imperial War Museum: 111 br. Kobal Collection: 19br (c Warner Brothers), 33br (c Columbia Pictures). London Features International: 113 bl. Mary Evans Picture Library: 4tl, 4cl, 4b, 9t, 9b, 10r, 15r, 17br, 18tl, 20br, 21t, 26bl, 22c, 26bl, 27t, 29l, 30tl, 32tl &bl, 33tl, 38l, 41bl, 42br & tl (detail) & 64 tl, 44br, 48bc, 50cl, 51br, 52l, 54br, 58tl, 59t, 62l, 62br, 63tr & br, 67br, 68c, 69b, 72t & b, 73cl, 75bl, 78cr, 79cr, 8ocl, 82b, 83t, 84t, 88br, 90b, 92bl & br, 94tl, 95br, 96 cr, 96bl & detail, 97br, 98t, 100tl & bc, 102tl, 103t & br, 106tl, cl, cr, 107tr & br, 108tl &c, 109cl & br, 112c, 113tr. Military Photo Library: 110bc (Crown Copyright - ABF Museum), 111tc (c) Geoff Lee, 112bl (c) Robin Adshead. National Maritime Museum (London): 58, 68b, 69t, 77bl, 84b, 85t, 86cl, 89t, 94br, 104c. National Gallery (Scotland): 61bc. National Portrait Gallery (London): 50tl, 53tr & br, 61r, 64tl, 67tr, 68t, 73tr, 80tl, 93r. Spectrum Colour Library: 53tr. The Master and Fellows of Corpus Christie College Cambridge: 53tl. National Railway Museum: 92t. Press Association: 98b. Ann Ronan/Image Select: 26tl, 31tr, 76tr, 89b, 99t. David Sellman (c): 12b. Spectrum Colour Library: 78bl, 83b.

Every effort has been made to trace the copyright holders and we apologise in advance for any unintentional omissions. We would be pleased to insert the appropriate acknowledgments in the next edition.